Morrisburg Ontario in Colour Photos, Saving Our History One Photo at a Time

Photography
by Barbara Raué
2016

Series Name:
Cruising Ontario

Book 156: Morrisburg

Cover photo: 50 Lakeshore Drive, Page 15

Series Name: Cruising Ontario
Saving Our History One Photo at a Time
in colour photos

Books Available in Alphabetical Order:
Aberfoyle, Acton, Alton, Amherstburg, Ancaster, Arthur, Aylmer, Ayr, Bloomingdale, Brantford, Burlington, Caledon, Caledonia, Cambridge, Clifford, Conestogo, Delhi, Dorchester to Aylmer, Drayton, Drumbo, Dundas, Eden Mills, Elmira, Elora, Essex, Fergus, Guelph, Hagersville, Hamilton, Hanover, Harriston, Hespeler, Jarvis, Kingston, Kingsville, Kitchener, Linwood, Listowel, London, Lucknow, Mono, Mount Forest, Neustadt, New Hamburg, Niagara-on-the-Lake, Oakville, Orangeville, Orillia, Owen Sound, Palmerston, Peterborough, Petrolia, Port Elgin, Preston, Rockwood, Sarnia, Seaforth, Sheffield, Shelburne, Simcoe, Southampton, St. Jacobs, St. Marys, St. Thomas, Stoney Creek, Stratford, Thamesford, Tillsonburg, Waterdown, Waterford, Waterloo, Welland, Wellesley, Windsor, Wingham, Woodstock

Book 114-116: Waterloo updated
Book 117-119: Windsor
Book 120-121: Amherstburg
Book 122: Essex
Book 123-124: Kingsville
Book 125-127: Woodstock
Book 128: Thamesford
Book 129-132: St. Marys
Book 133-136: Sarnia
Book 137: Petrolia
Book 138-139: Welland
Book 140-145: Kingston
Book 146-149: Ottawa
Book 150-151: Midland

Book 152: Penetanguishene
Book 153: Kemptville
Book 154: Cornwall
Book 155: Mariatown to Maitland
Book 156: Morrisburg

Other Books by Barbara Raue

Coins of Gold

Arrows, Indians and Love

The Life and Times of Barbara
Volume 1: Inventions That Have Enhanced My Life
Volume 2: Entertainment That I Have Enjoyed
Volume 3: East Coast Trips
Volume 4: Olympics Have Always Intrigued Me
Volume 5: Wonders of the World
Volume 6: Caribbean Cruises We Have Enjoyed
Volume 7: Animals
Volume 8: Storms and Other Major Disasters in My Lifetime
Volume 9: Wars, Terrorist Attacks and Major Disasters

The Cromwell Family Book

Laura Secord Discovered

Daddy Where Are You?

Montana Series
Book 1: Montana Dream
Book 2: Life on the Montana Frontier
Book 3: Montana to Boston and Back

Visit Barbara's website to view all of her books
http://barbararaue.ca

Table of Contents

In 1997, Morrisburg was amalgamated with the Village of Iroquois, Matilda and Williamsburg Townships into the Township of South Dundas, in the United Counties of Stormont, Dundas and Glengarry along the north shore of the St. Lawrence River. The county was named in 1792 to honour Henry Dundas, who was Lord Advocate for Scotland and Colonial Secretary at the time. Matilda and Williamsburgh were two of Upper Canada's original eight Royal Townships.

On November 11, 1813, the Battle of Crysler's Farm, at which a British force repelled an invading American army, took place near here. United Empire Loyalists settled in Dundas County creating West Williamsburg; it was part of the Williamsburg Canal project. Between 1843 and 1856, canals were built on the north side of the St. Lawrence River. West Williamsburg was renamed Morrisburg in 1851 in honour of Brockville politician, James Morris, who was the first Postmaster General of the United Provinces of Canada. By 1860, Morrisburg had a growing manufacturing base consisting of a gristmill, a carding mill and a fanning mill. The Grand Trunk Railroad reached Morrisburg in 1855. A hydroelectric power plant was built in 1901.

During the 1950s, portions of Morrisburg were relocated because of expected flooding which would occur with the St. Lawrence Seaway project. Over eighty homes were moved and the entire downtown business district was demolished and relocated in a shopping plaza. The Canadian National Railway line was moved about a kilometre north of its original location. Much of the former rail bed was used for reconstructing Highway 2. Buildings and other artefacts were moved and assembled to create Upper Canada Village, a tribute to the area's pioneers.

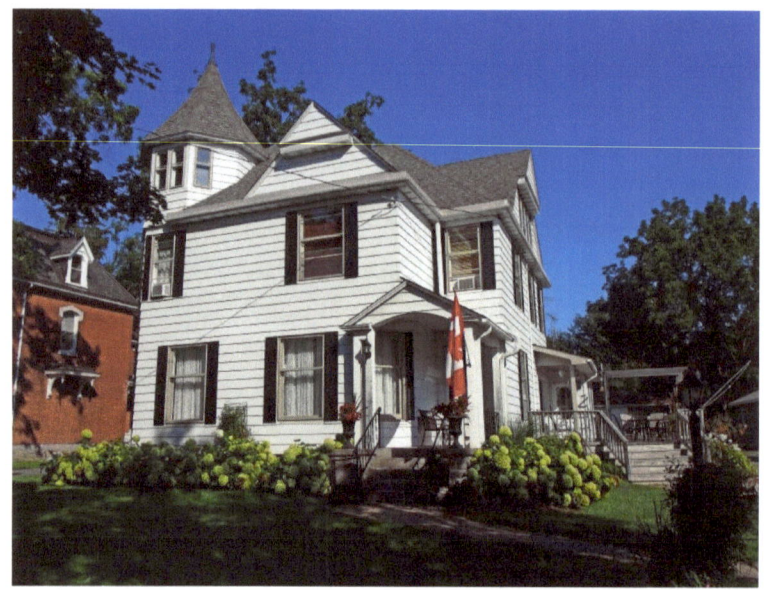

12 Lakeshore Drive – Queen Anne Revival – irregular massing, steep hip roof, offset tower – original wood cladding has been covered with modern siding

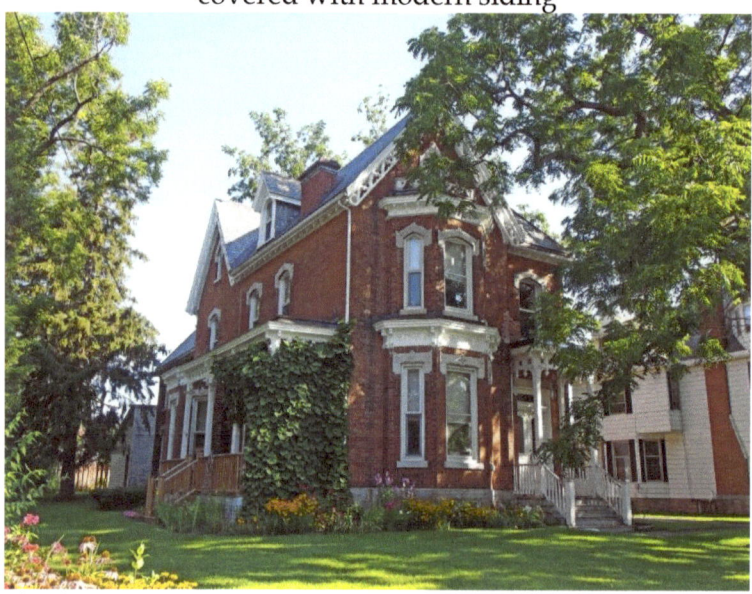

14 Lakeshore Drive – Gothic Revival – built c. 1850 - steeply pitched slate roof, verge board trim on gables, narrow windows in the bay windows emphasize the vertical

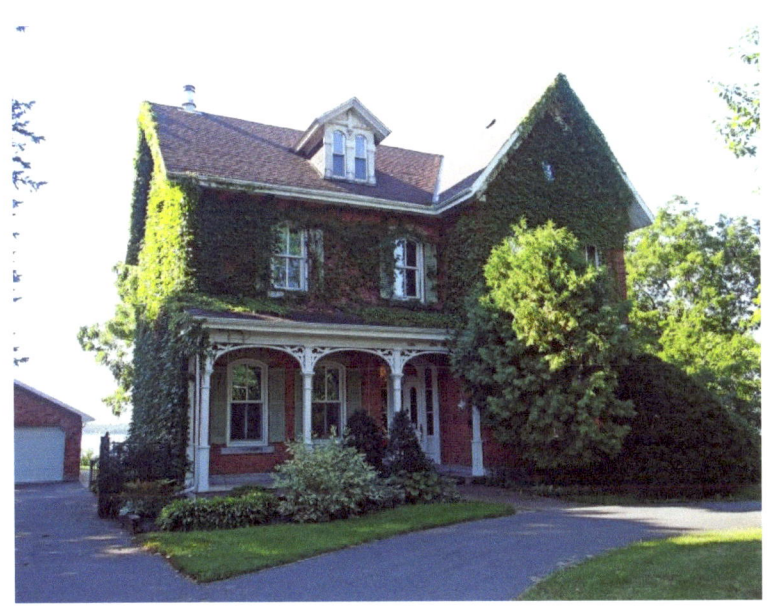

17 Lakeshore Drive – Ontario Vernacular - a hybrid, typical of
this period – built 1858 - sidelights

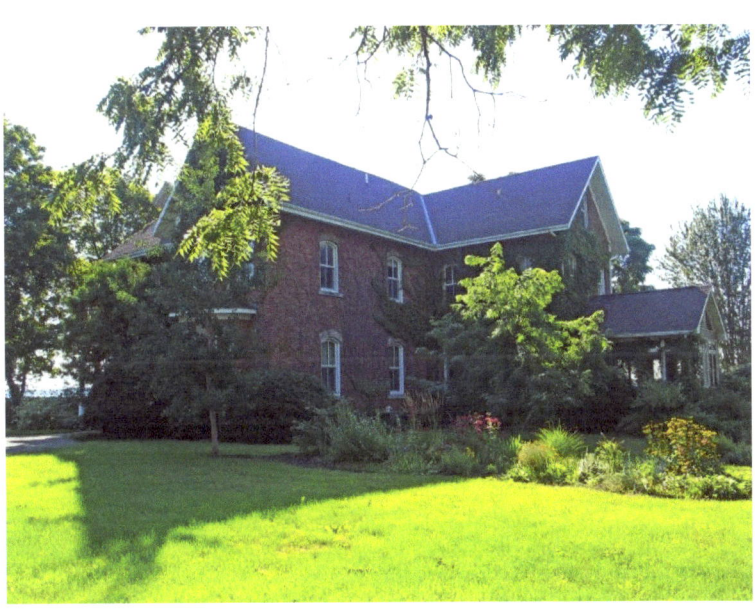

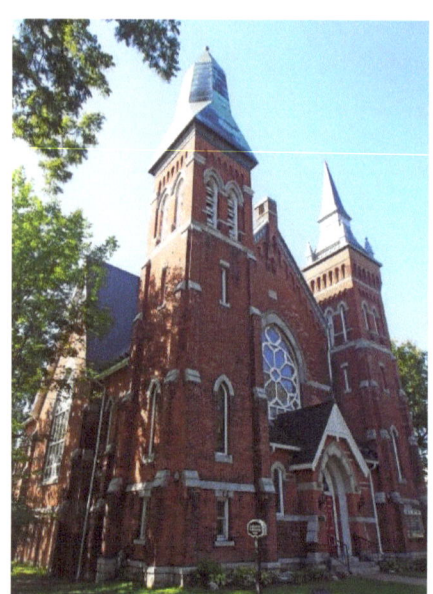 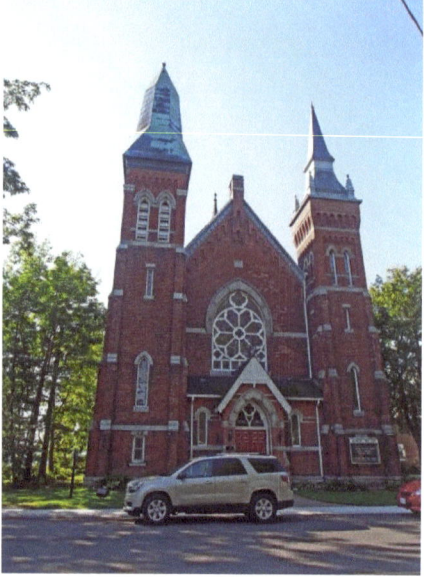

Lakeshore Drive United Church – built 1880 – Gothic – brick with cut stone dressings – rose windows, buttresses, finials on east tower (towers are not symmetrical), lancet windows

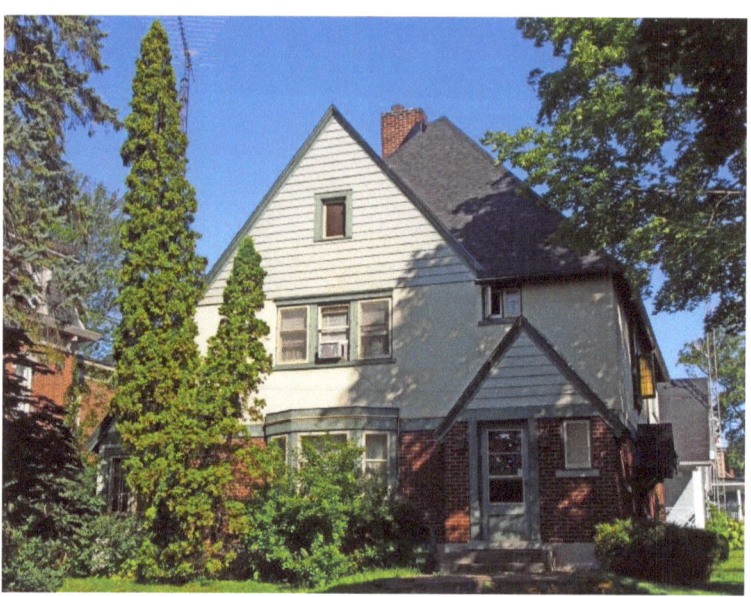

20 Lakeshore Drive – Vernacular – bay window

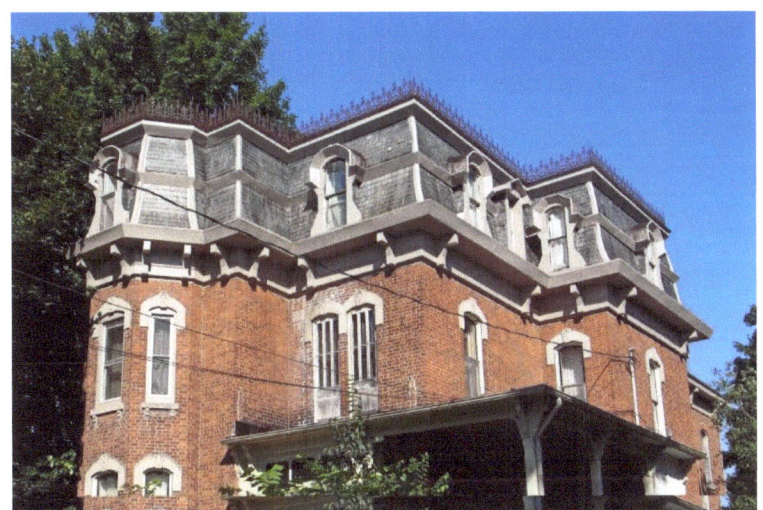

22 Lakeshore Drive – Second Empire – built 1879 – mansard roof, rounded dormers, heavy cornice brackets

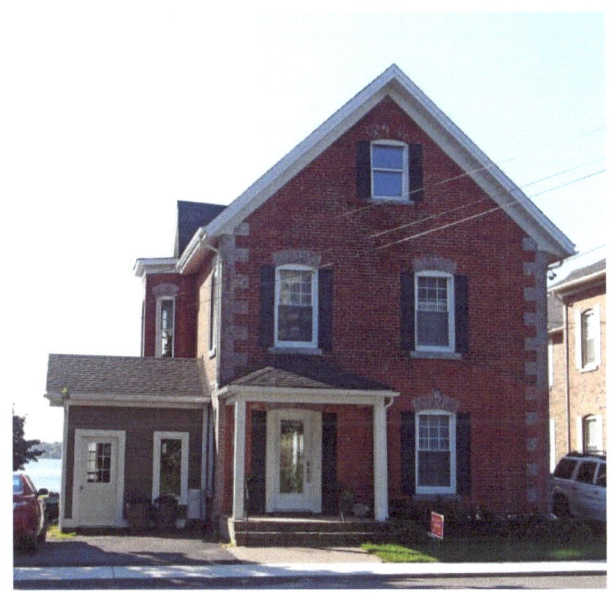

25 Lakeshore Drive – Gothic, corner quoins

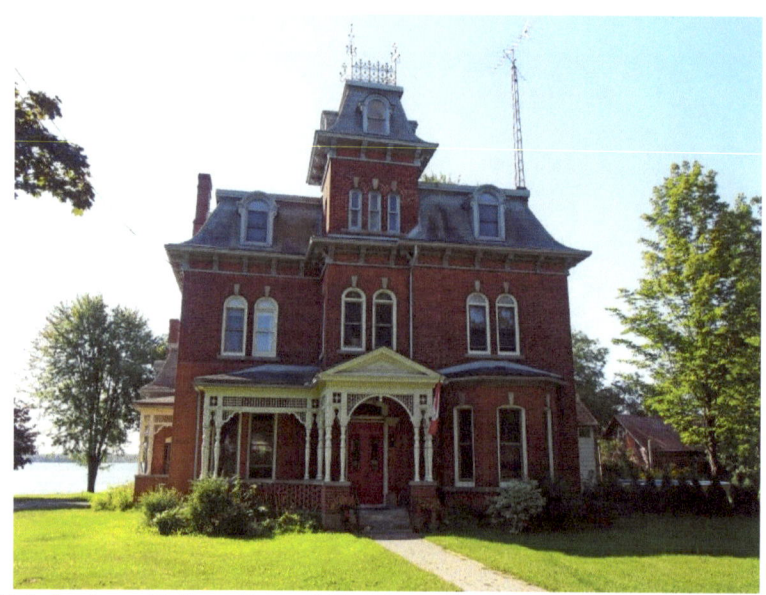

31 Lakeshore Drive – Second Empire style – projecting central tower, concave mansard roof, dormers; has eighteen stained glass windows, each with a different color scheme

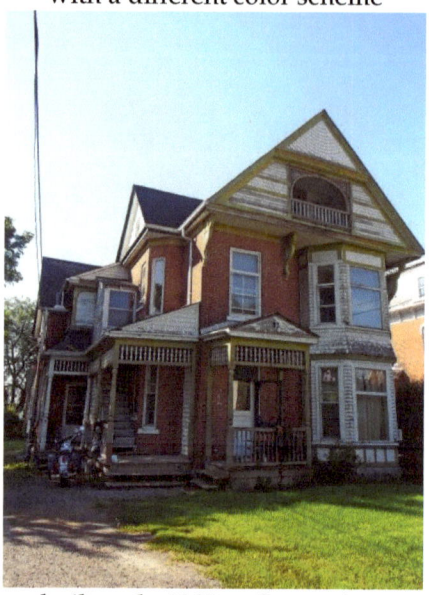

33 Lakeshore Drive – built early 1880s – Queen Anne style – steep hipped roof, angular bays – porches with spindle work, front gable clad with fish scale shingles arranged in a variety of patterns; separated by a series of horizontal cross-pieces which accent the balcony that is built into the gable

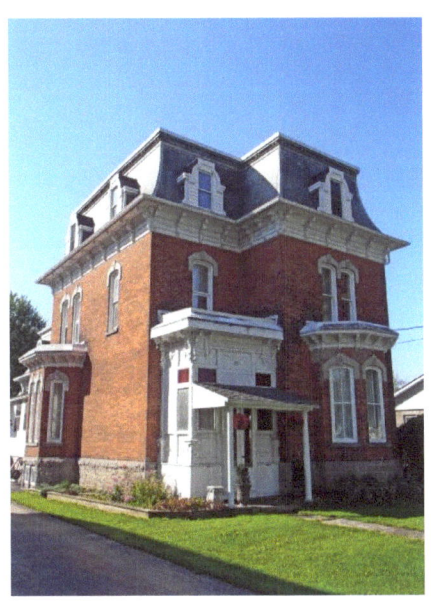

35 Lakeshore Drive – Second Empire style – built 1878 - concave slope to the slate mansard roof, mansard dormers, ornately bracketed eaves, one storey bay window; enclosed glazed vestibule

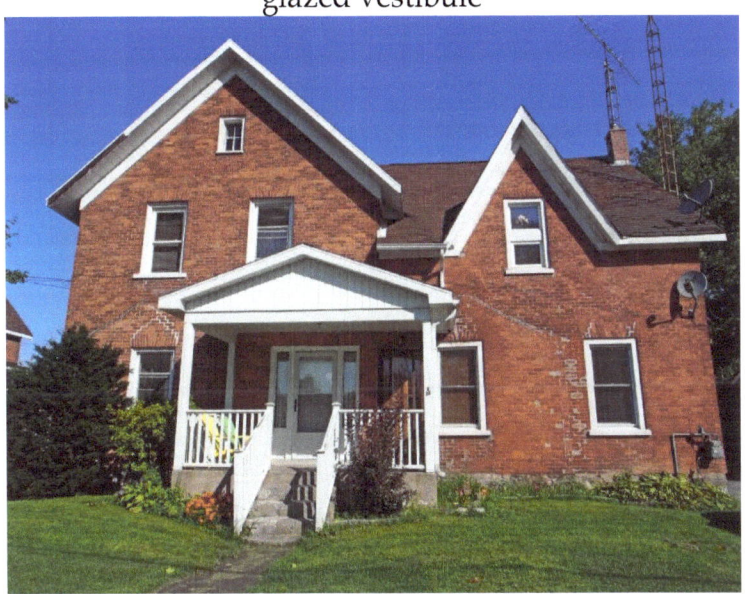

34 Lakeshore Drive – Victorian - sidelights

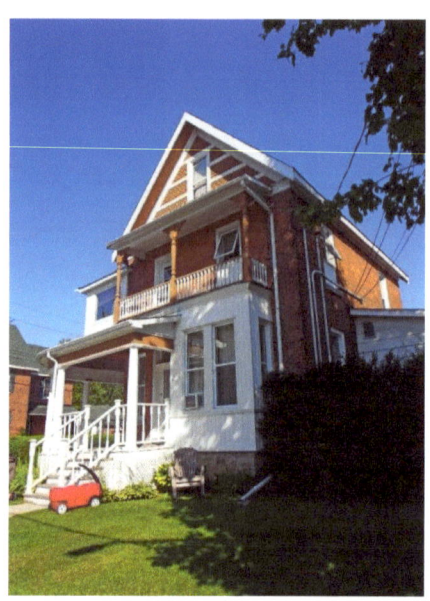

Lakeshore Drive - a series of horizontal cross-pieces in the gable, second floor veranda with decorative wood-turned spindles and open railing

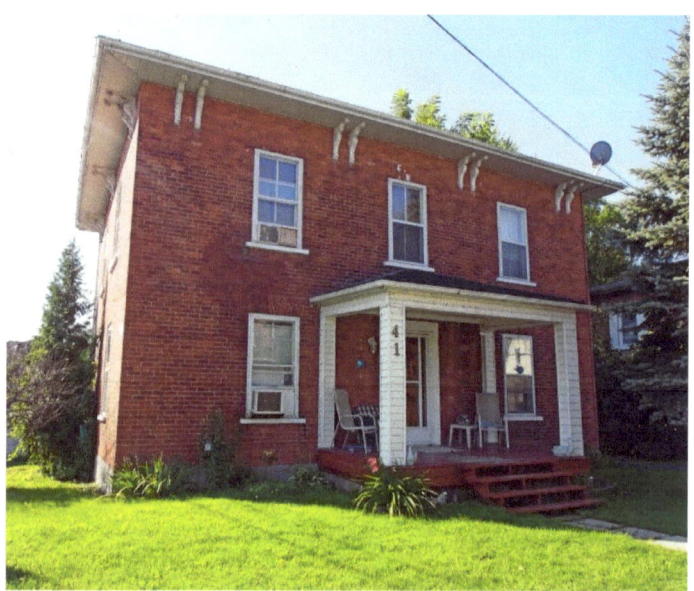

41 Lakeshore Drive – Italianate, paired cornice brackets

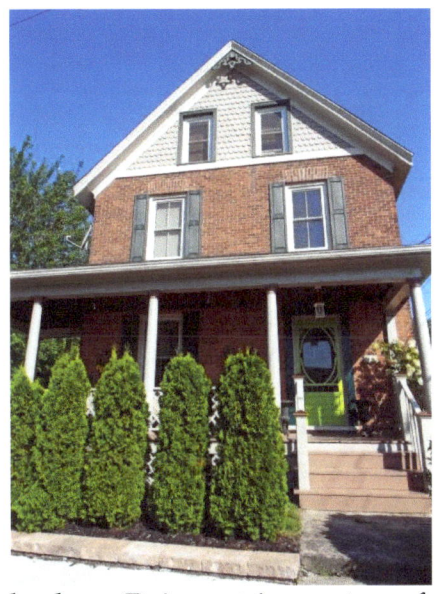

40 Lakeshore Drive – trim on top of gable

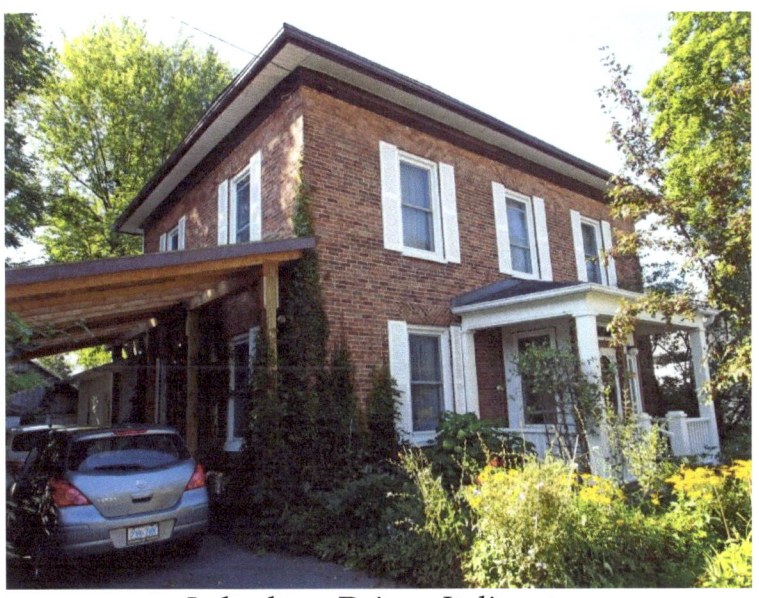

Lakeshore Drive - Italianate

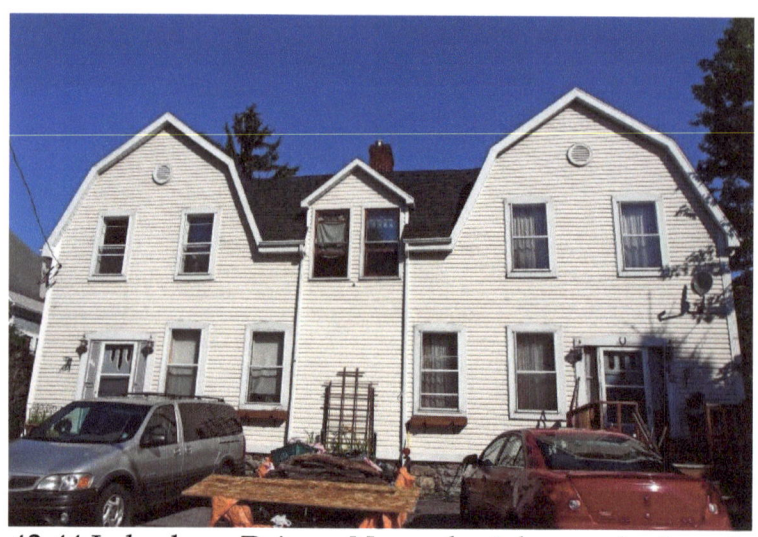

42-44 Lakeshore Drive – Neo-colonial – gambrel roofs

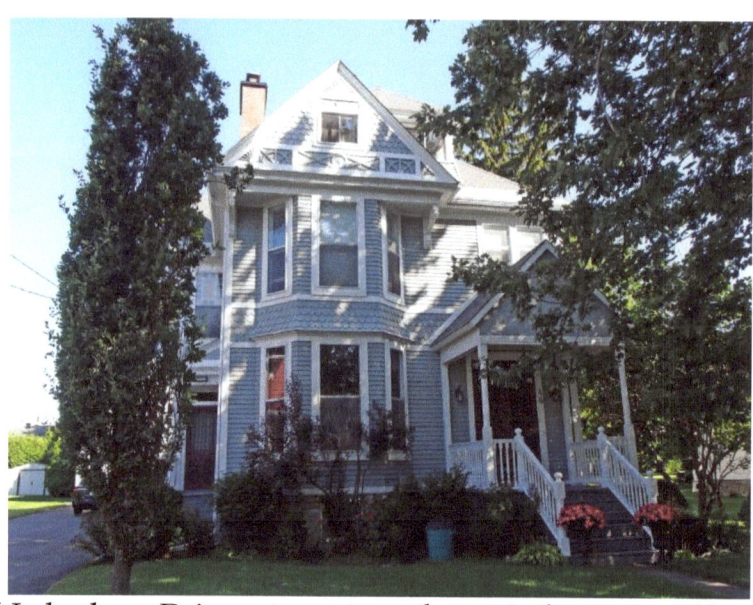

46 Lakeshore Drive – two-storey bay window topped by an intricately patterned gable; fish scale shingle patterning between first and second storeys; pediment above door, turned porch supports, open railing

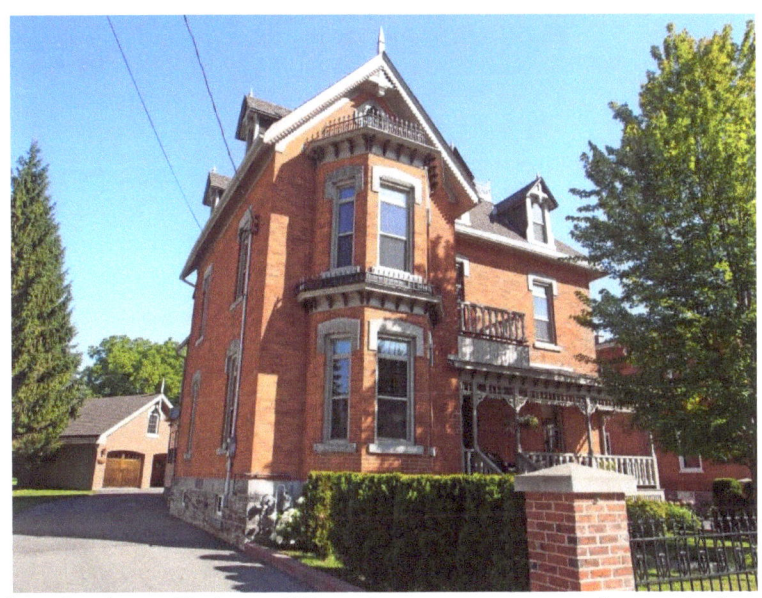

50 Lakeshore Drive – Victorian – two-storey bay windows with iron cresting above, widow's walk balcony on rooftop with iron cresting, dormers with finials; verandah with ornate capital detailing on the support posts with spindles under the cornice

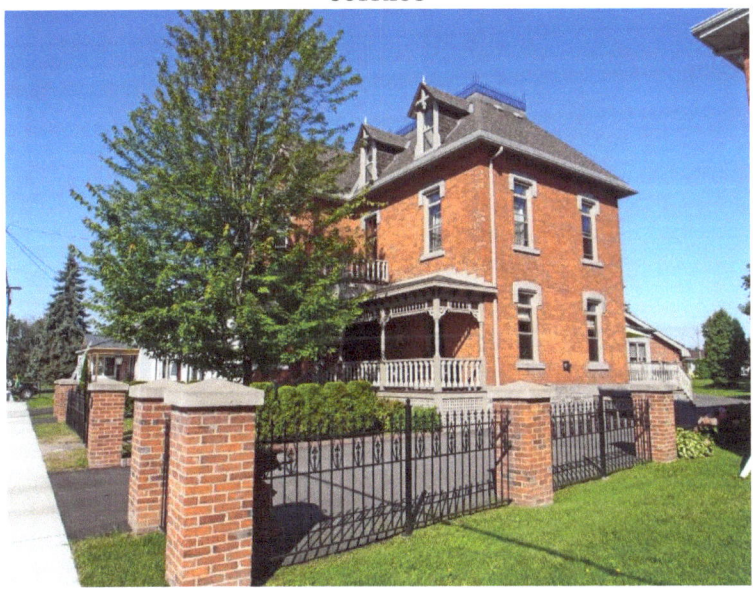

Inside 50 Lakeshore Drive

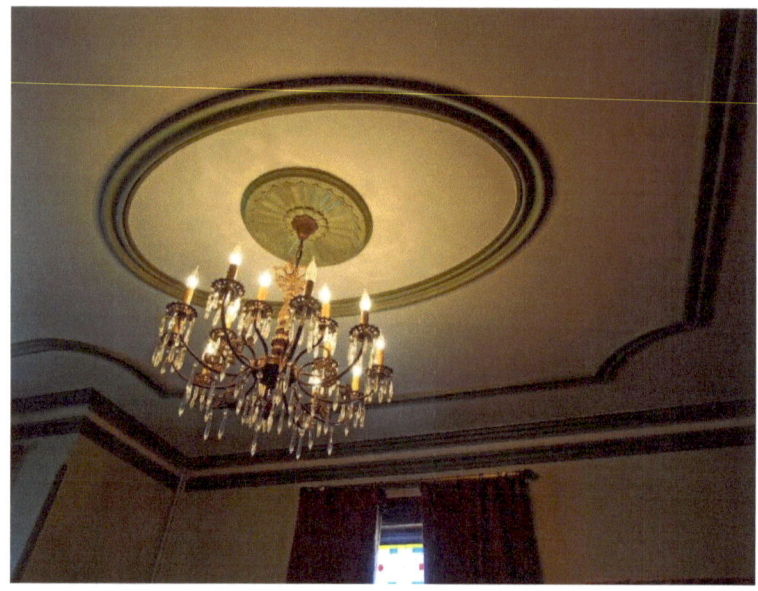

Restored crown molding and light fixture mounts

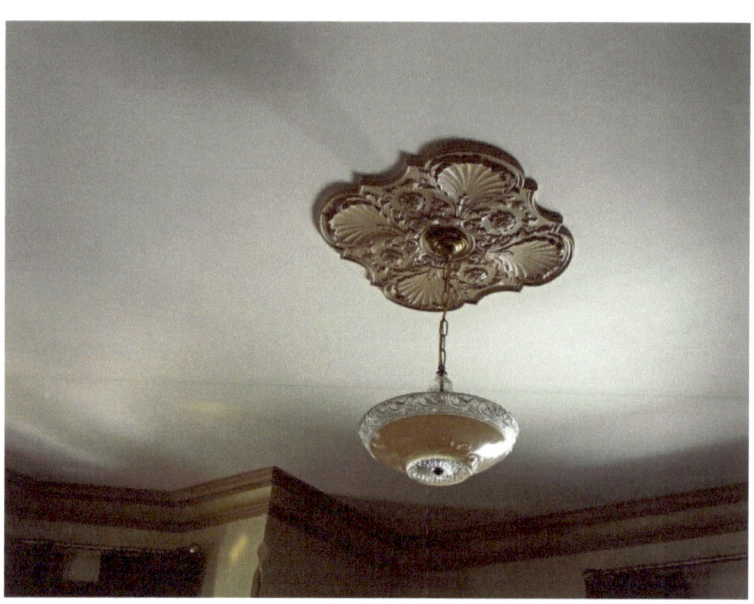

50 Lakeshore Drive

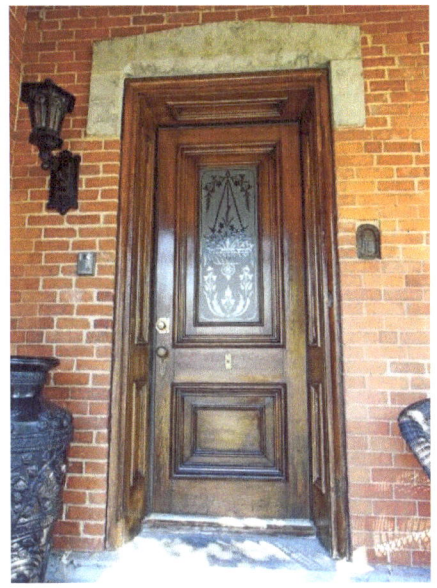

Original door restored

Inside 50 Lakeshore Drive

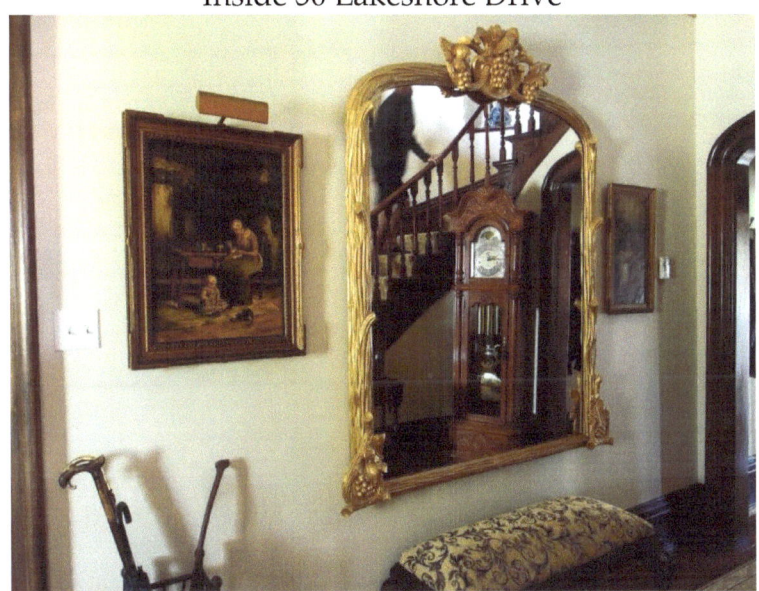

Banister for stairs restored – seen through mirror

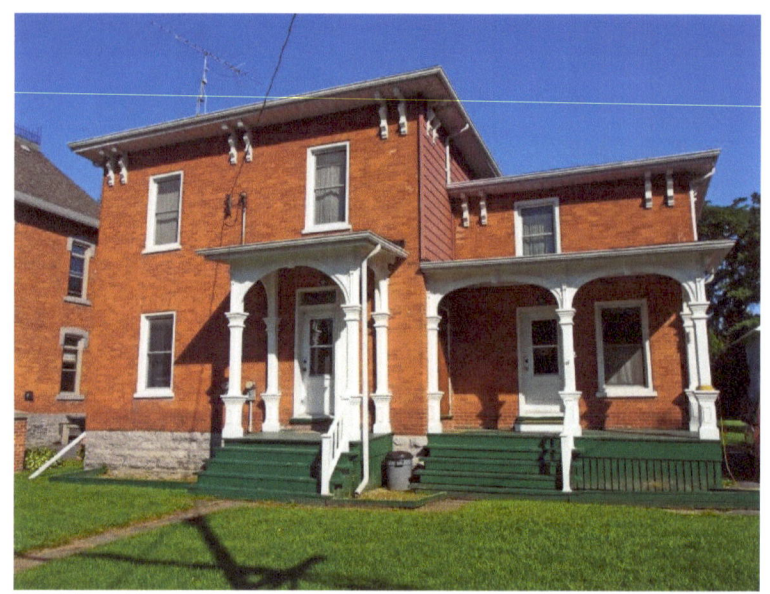

48 Lakeshore Drive – Italianate, paired cornice brackets, decorative porch and verandah supports; transom

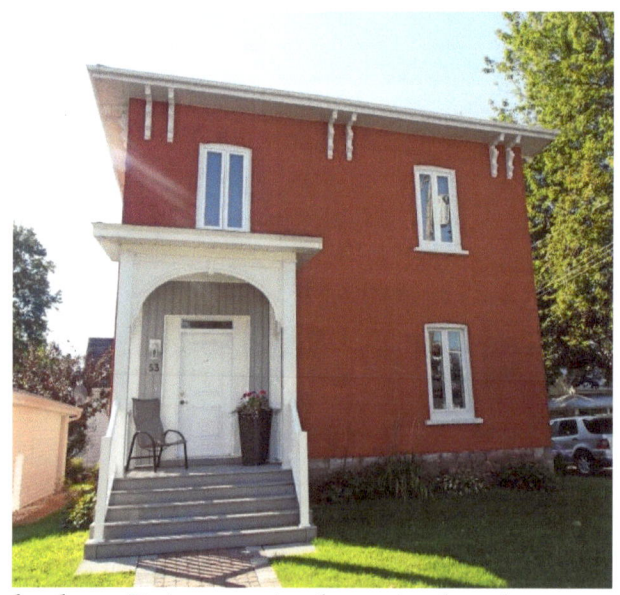

53 Lakeshore Drive – paired cornice brackets, transom

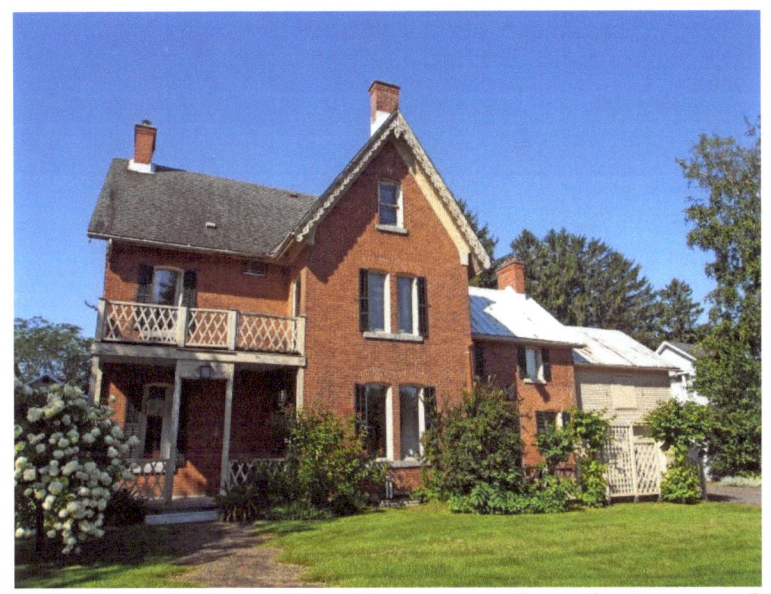

80 Lakeshore Drive – Victorian – verge board trim on gable, second floor balcony with open railing

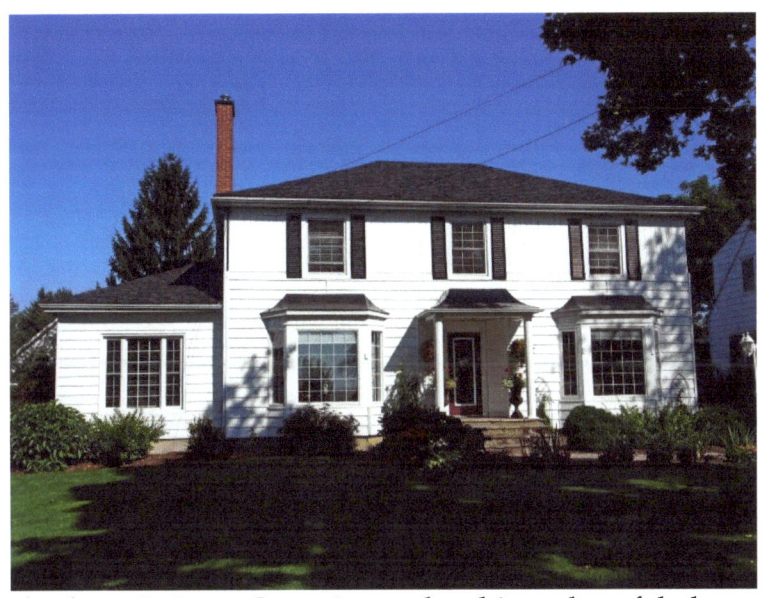

Lakeshore Drive – Georgian style – hipped roof, balanced façade, bay windows

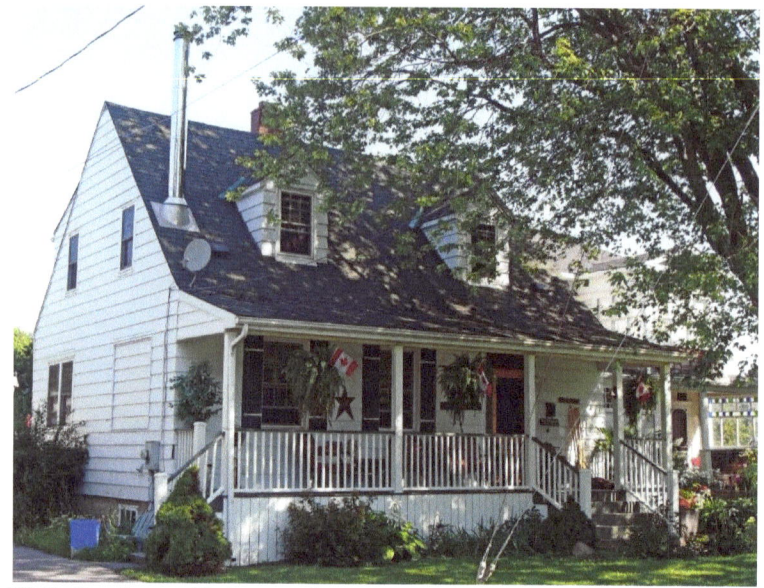

72 Lakeshore Drive – dormers; open railing on veranda

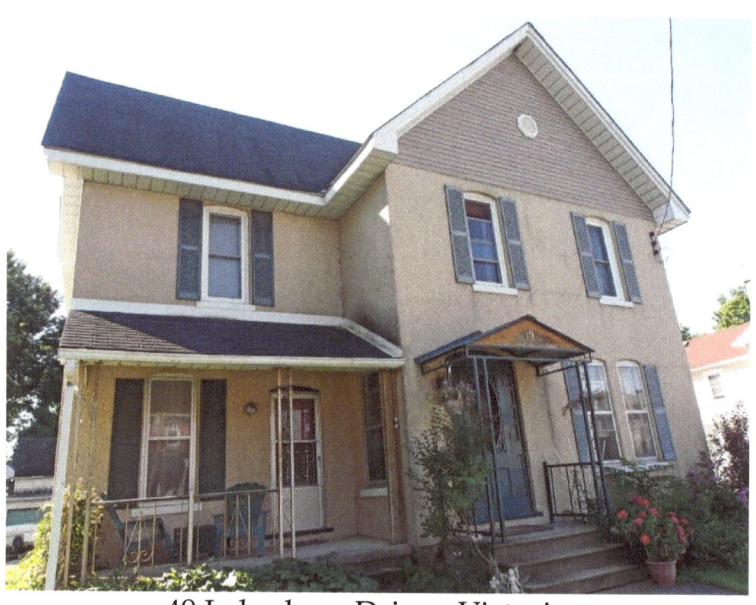

49 Lakeshore Drive - Victorian

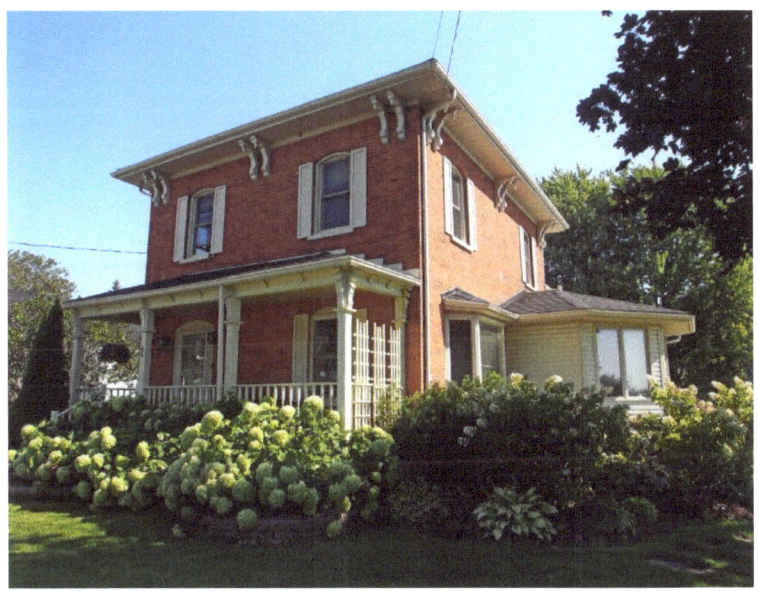

1 Augusta Street – Italianate – paired cornice brackets

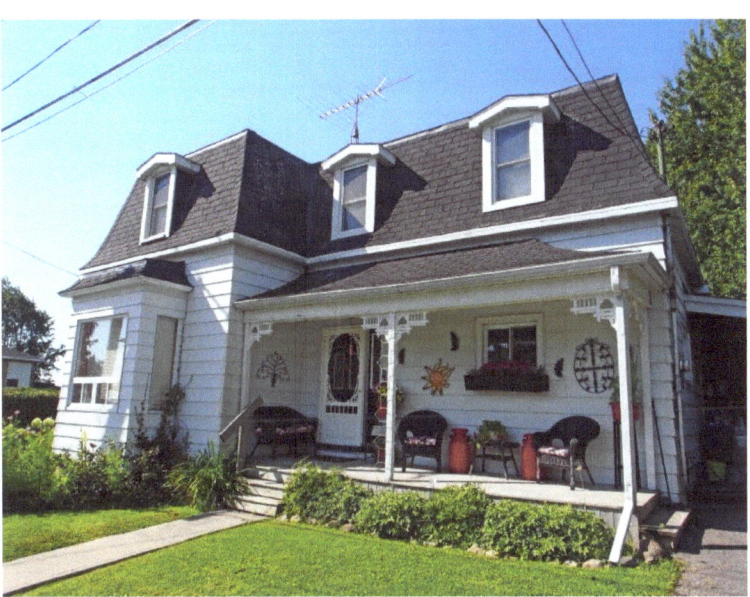

8 Augusta Street – mansard roof with dormers but not the intricate design of Second Empire style

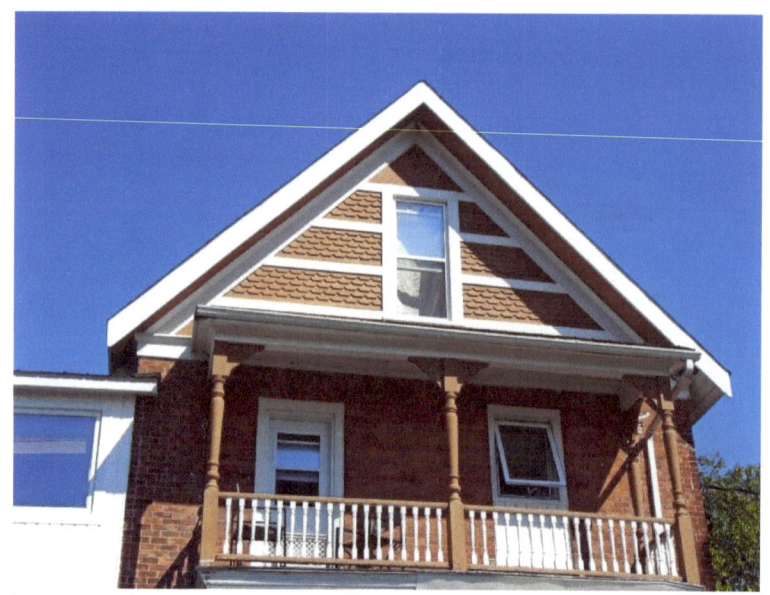

Augusta Street – second floor verandah with decorative wood-turned spindles and open railing; gable above with a series of horizontal cross-pieces

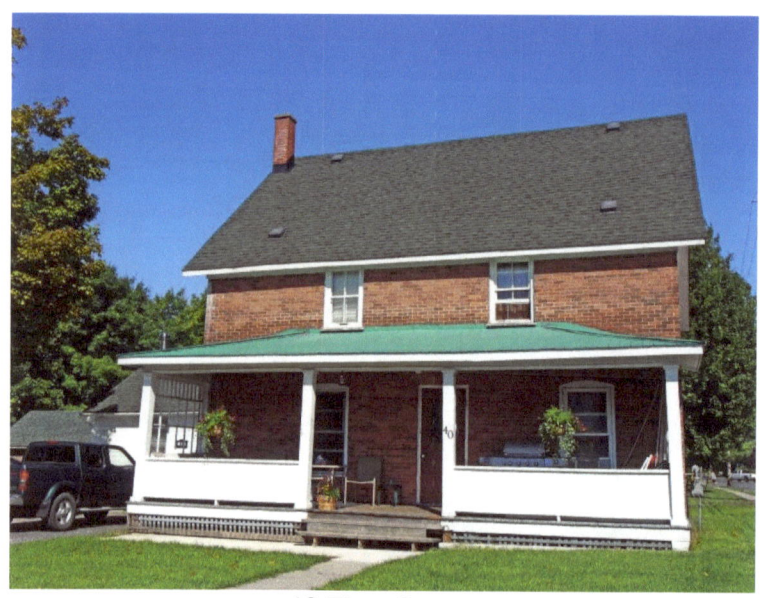

40 First Street

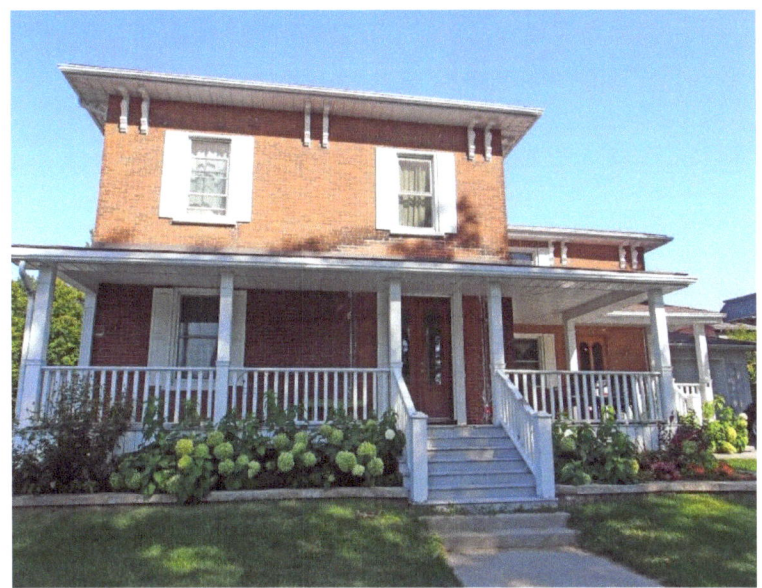

38 First Street – Italianate – paired cornice brackets, deep verandah with square support posts and open railing

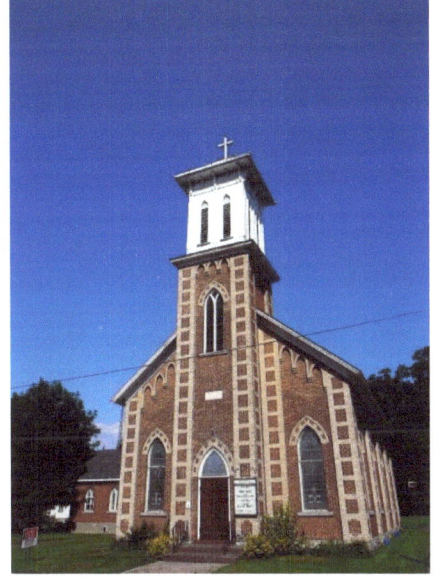

First Street – St. Paul's Lutheran Church – built 1895 – Gothic Revival design – polychrome brickwork to highlight and outline its façade; tower capped by a tall, wooden belfry with a shallow roof

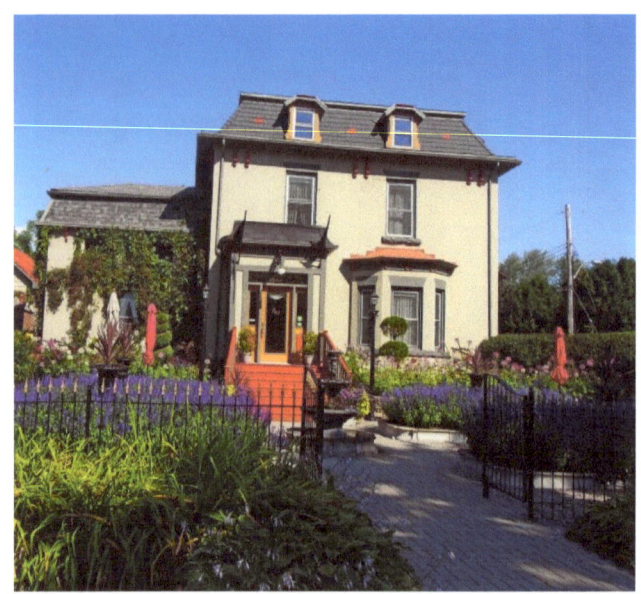

36 First Street – Russell Manor Bed and Breakfast – Second Empire style, mansard roof, cornice brackets, patterned slate roof, bay window

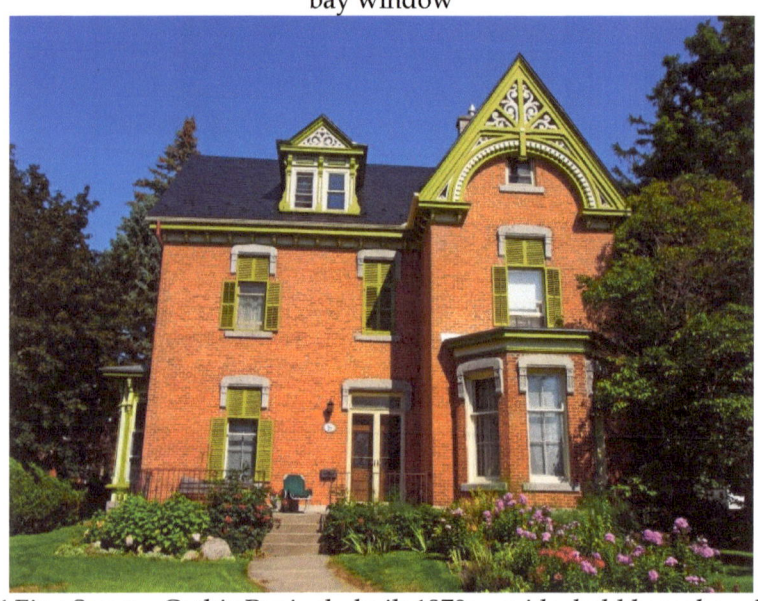

16 First Street – Gothic Revival - built 1870s – wide, bold bargeboards, central pinnacle suspended beneath the peak ending in a knob-like pendant above the third floor window; intricate cut-out patterns adorning the gable ends

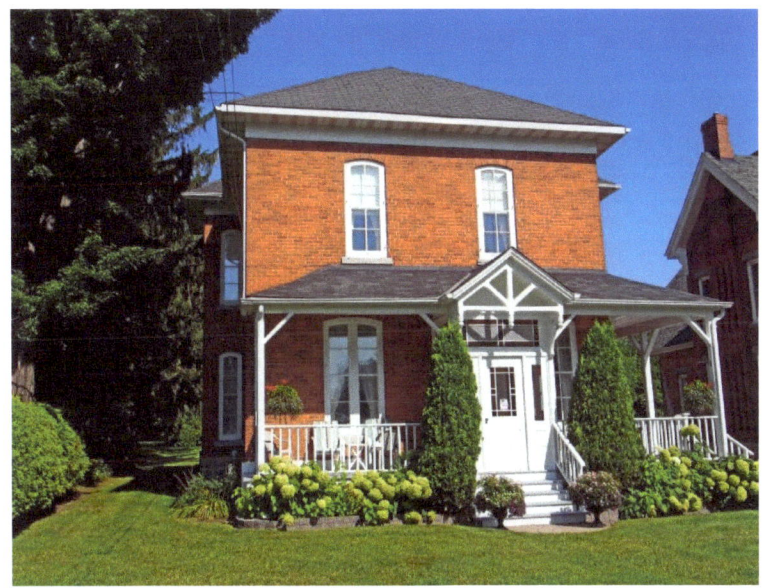

14 First Street – Italianate – c. 1860 – hipped roof

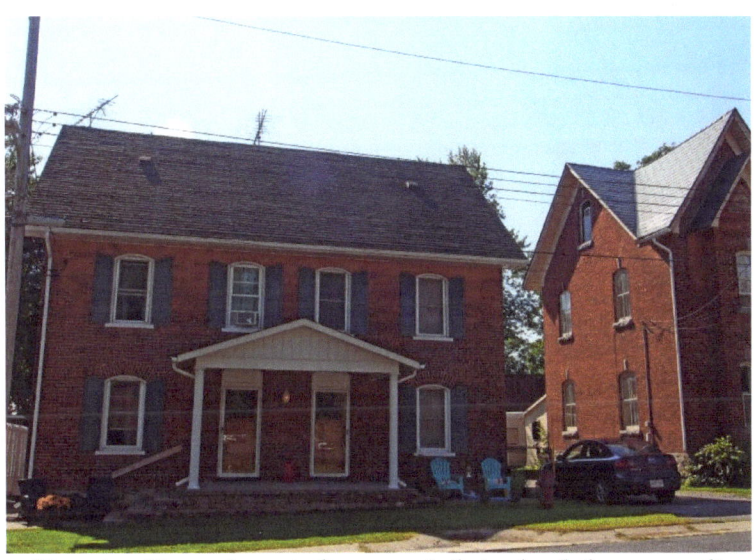

First Street – Georgian style - semi-detached, large pediment over doors

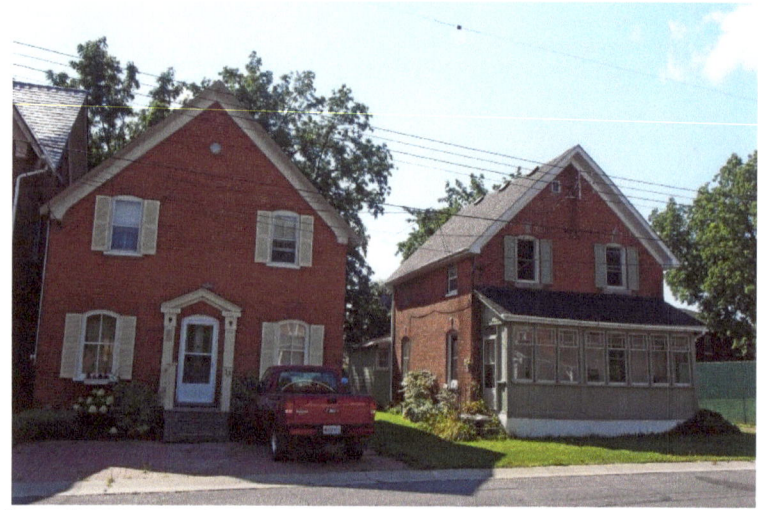

13 and 15 First Street – Victorian - #13 has open pediment above door and engaged columns; #15 has enclosed porch

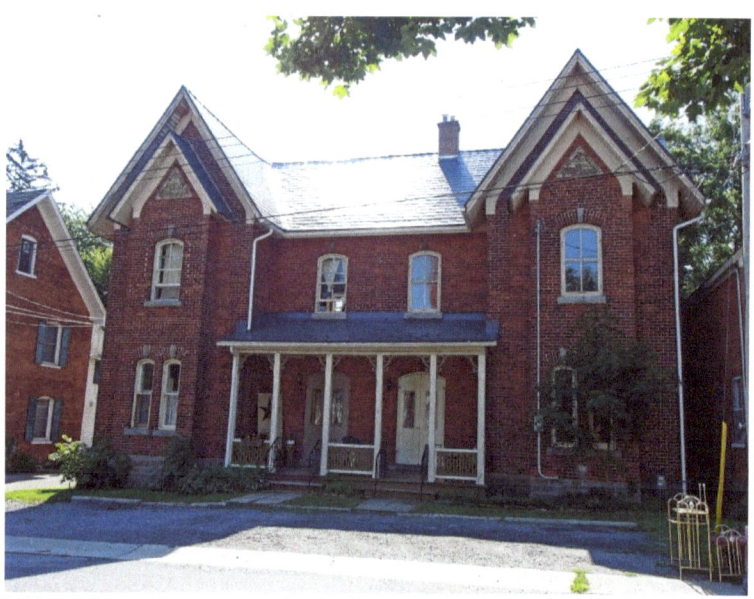

9-11 First Street – semi-detached – built 1881 – Gothic Revival style – six slender posts supporting the porch contributed to the vertical feel of the houses; the brackets and balustrades of the porch retain the decorative flair associated with this style

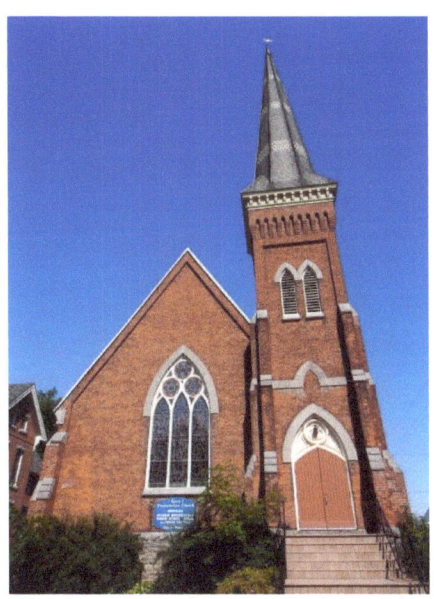

First Street – Knox Presbyterian Church - Gothic style - built in 1879 - red brick with cut stone dressings; roof and broach spire are covered with patterned slate; buttresses; lancet windows, beveled dentil molding

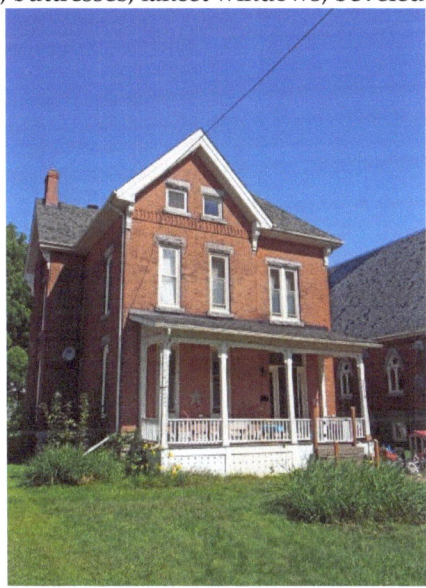

12 First Street – Gothic Revival – built 1870 – purchased as a manse in 1906; soldier style stone lintels; cornice brackets; decorative support posts on veranda, open railing

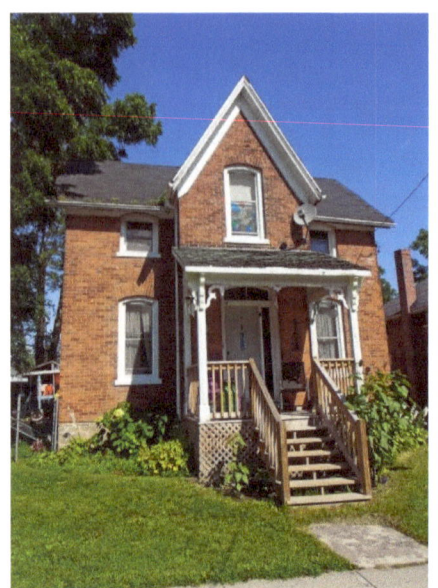

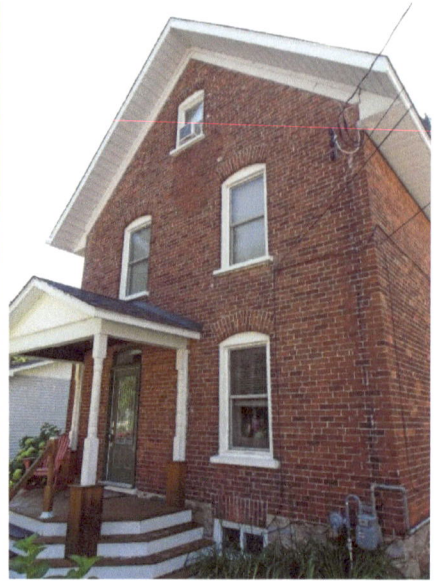

First Street – Gothic decorative support posts, open railing, sidelights, transom

Victorian – pediment, turned porch support posts

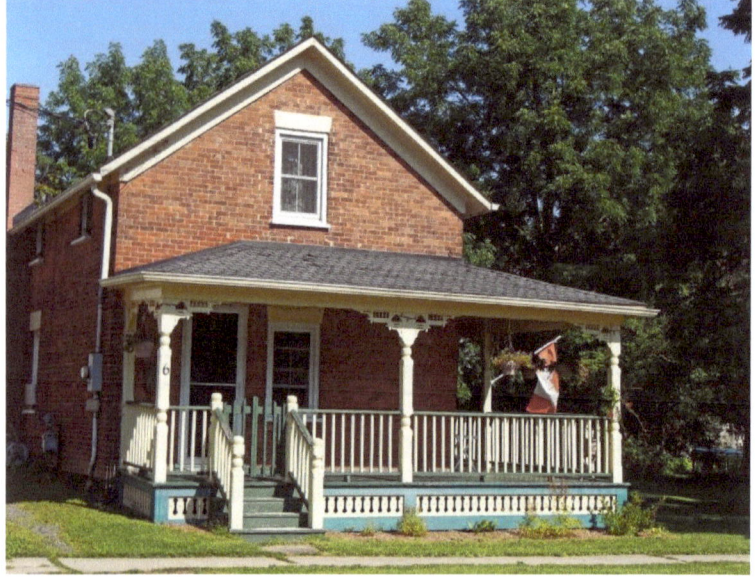

6 First Street – built in the 1850s, one of the oldest houses in Morrisburg; low pitched roof; open railing on veranda

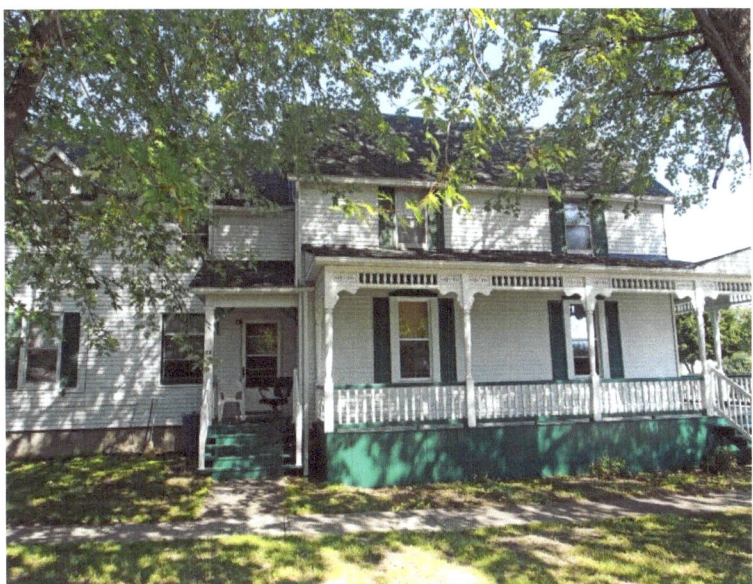

2 First Street – Gothic– built 1876 – spacious front porch supported on seven well-turned columns; spindles along the porch roof and the balusters that support the railing add contrast to the main horizontal emphasis of the clapboard siding

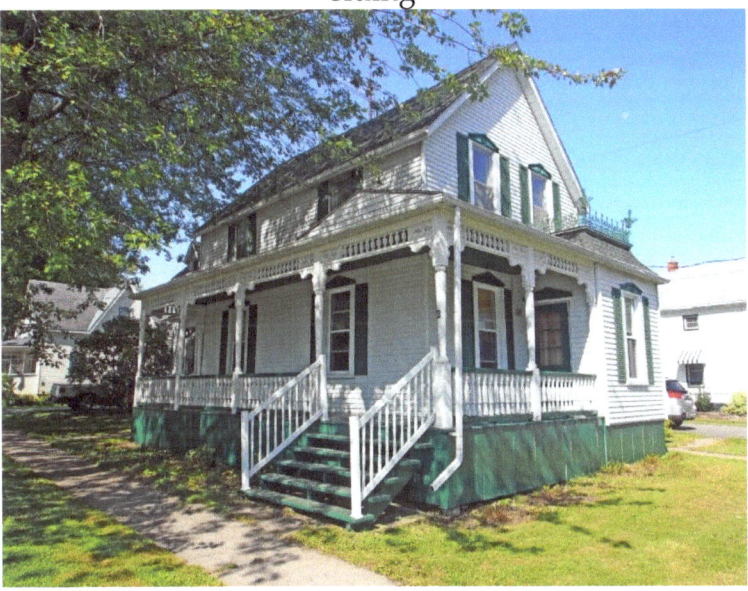

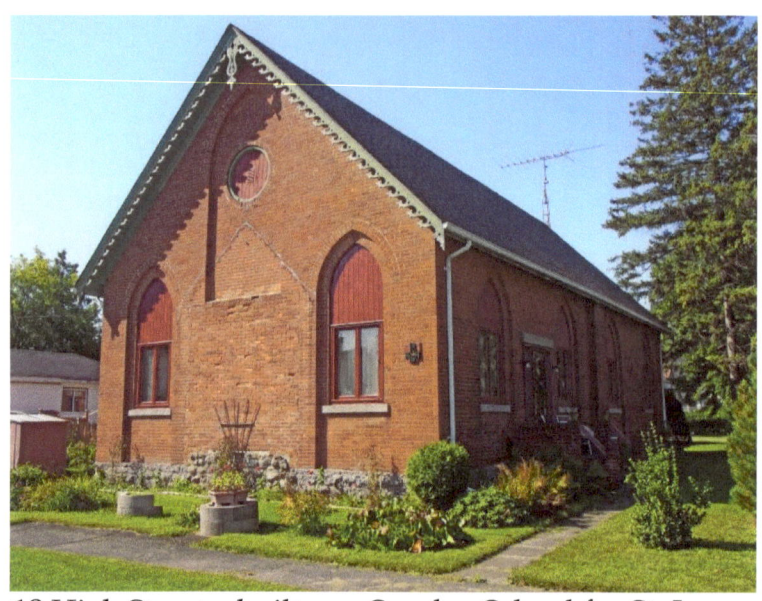

18 High Street – built as a Sunday School for St. James Anglican Church in 1905 – converted into a private home in the 1970s

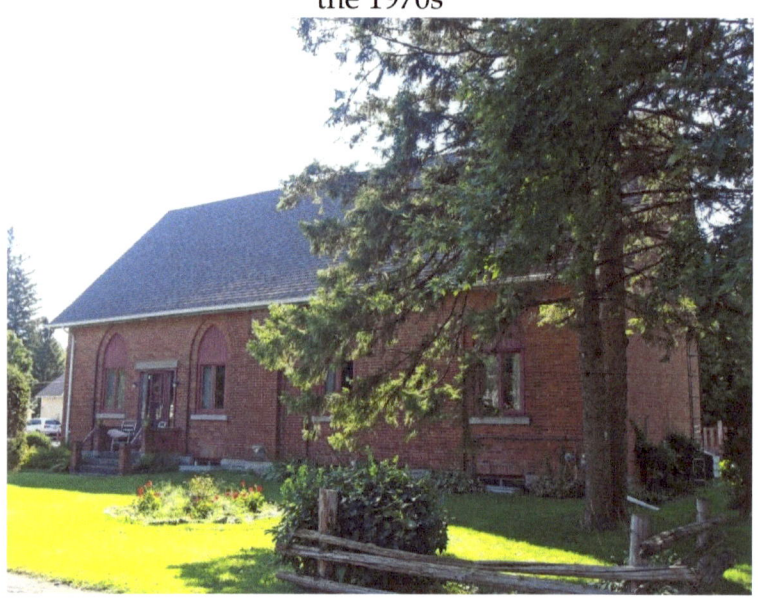

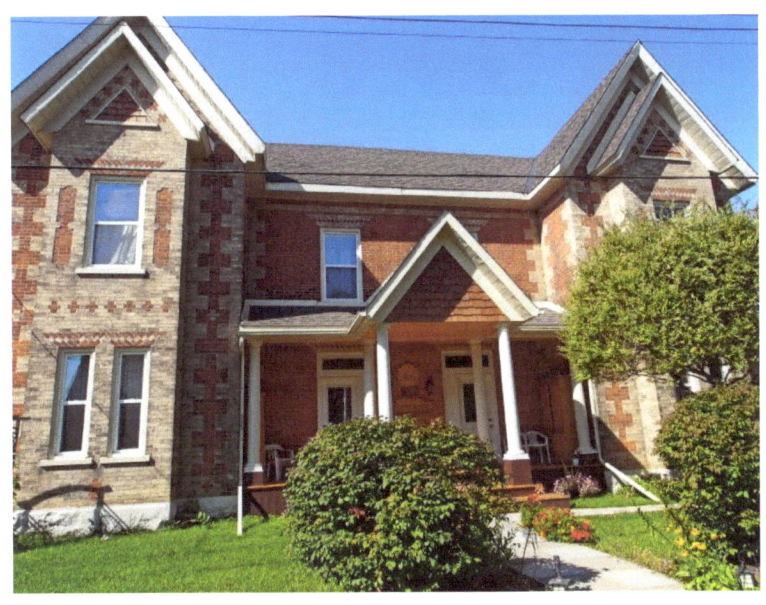

24 High Street – Gothic Revival style – symmetrical organization, steeply pitched roof gables, tall twin window bays; dichromatic brickwork; transom windows

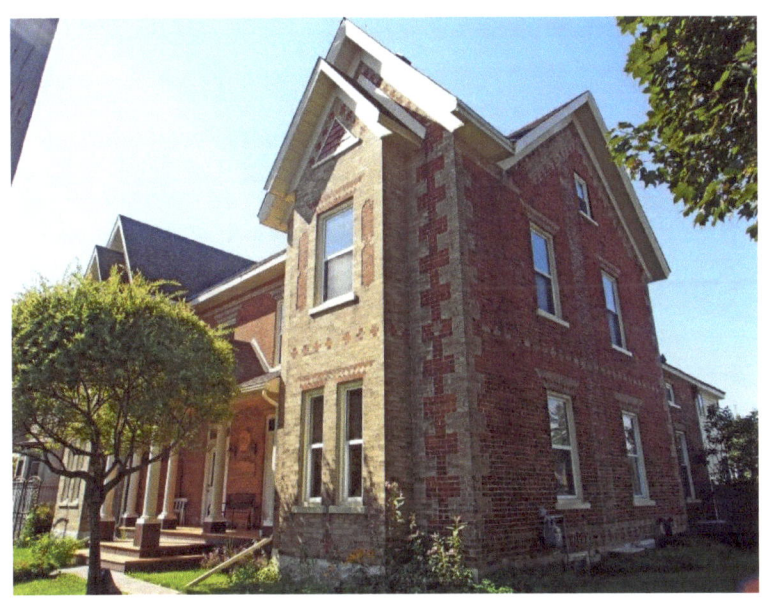

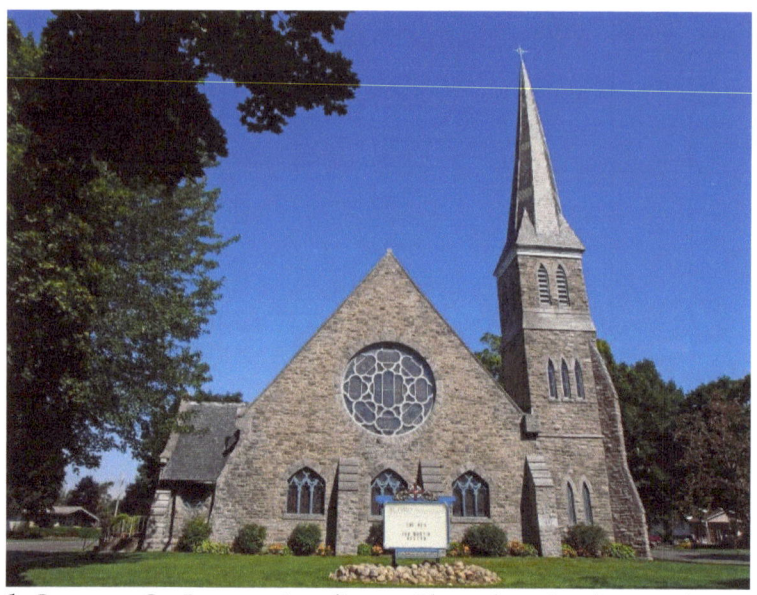

High Street – St. James Anglican Church – Gothic style – built 1893 – bell tower remains from previous building built in 1857 – slate-covered roof and tower; rose window, buttresses

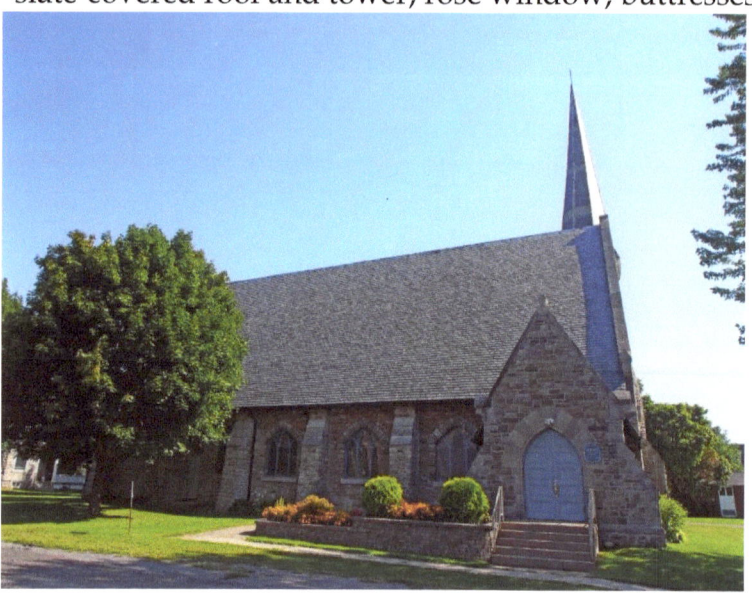

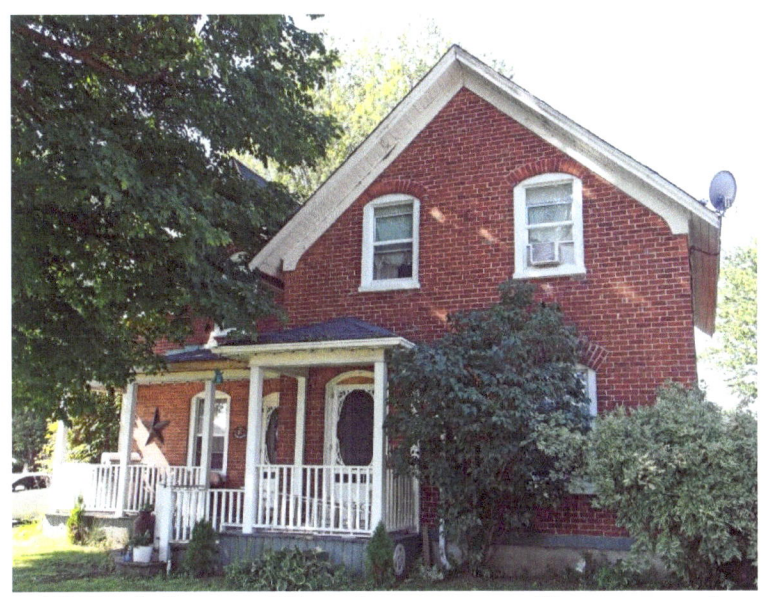

72 High Street – Victorian – open railing on porch

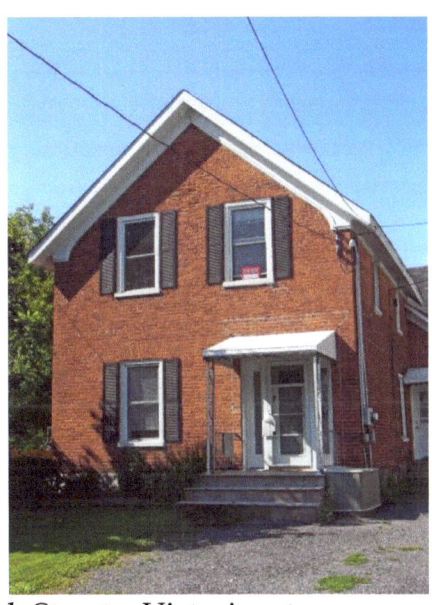

66 High Street – Victorian, transom window

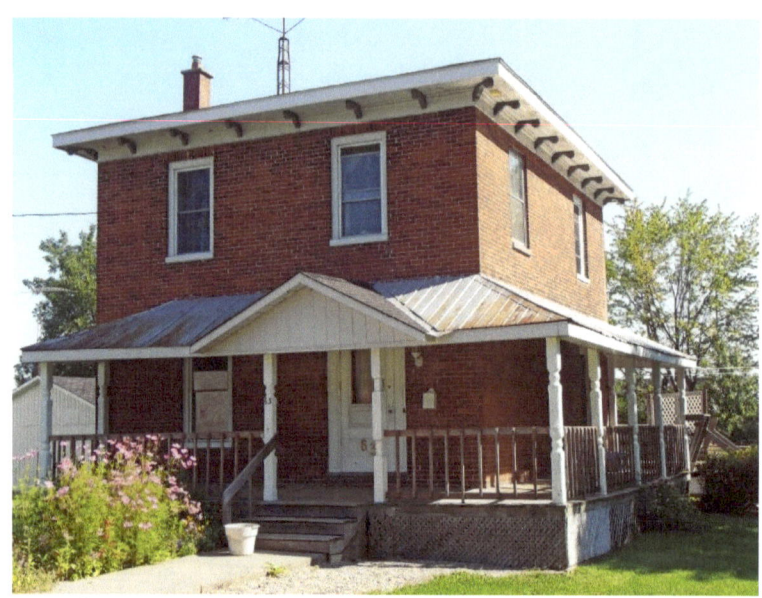

63 High Street – Italianate – hipped roof, cornice brackets, turned spindle wraparound veranda supports, open railing

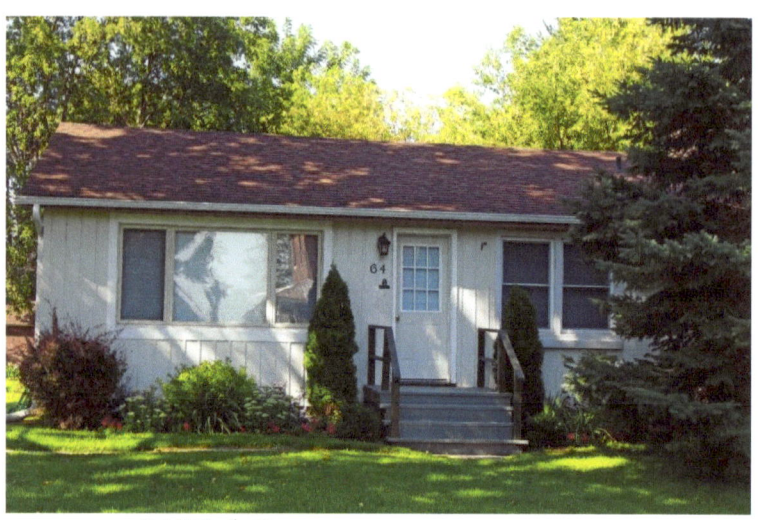

64 High Street – one storey cottage

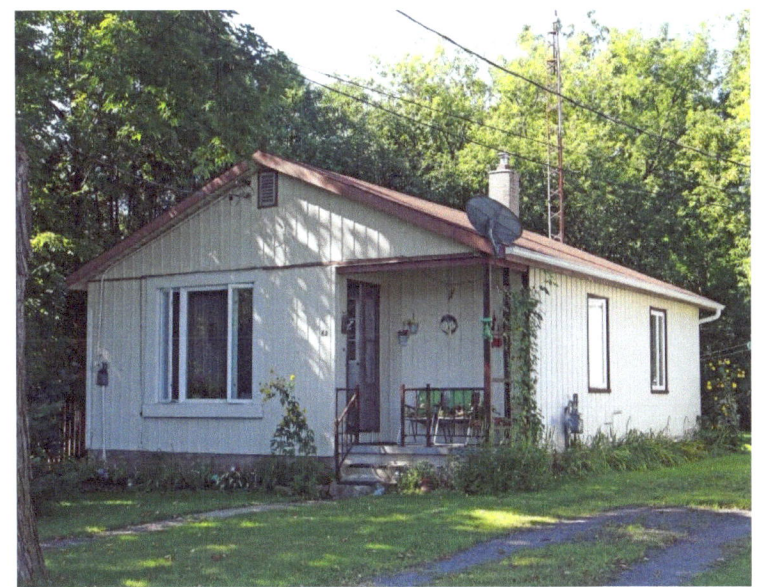

62 High Street

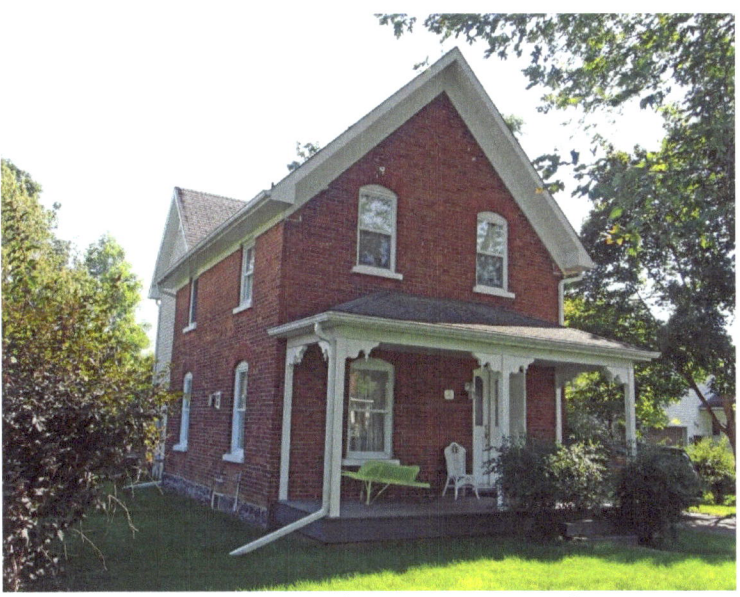

61 High Street – Victorian – decorative veranda support posts

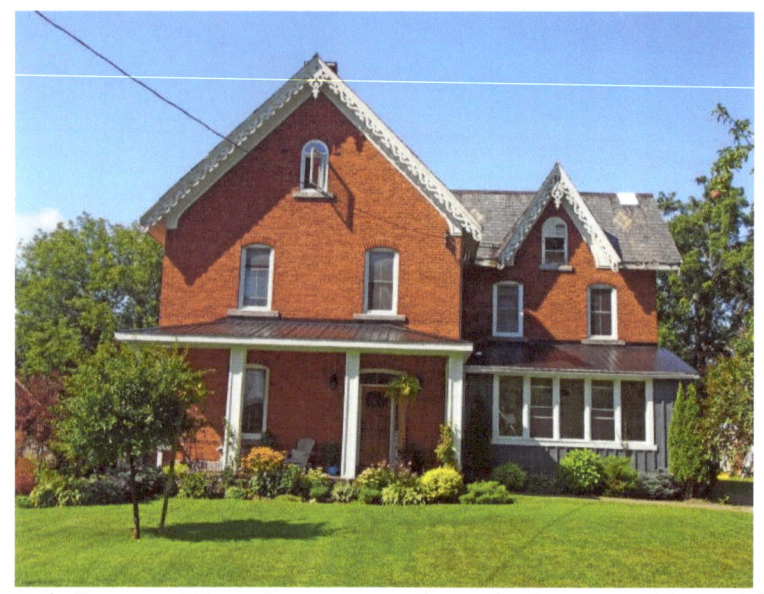

High Street – Victorian – verge board trim on gables with finials, open veranda, transom window

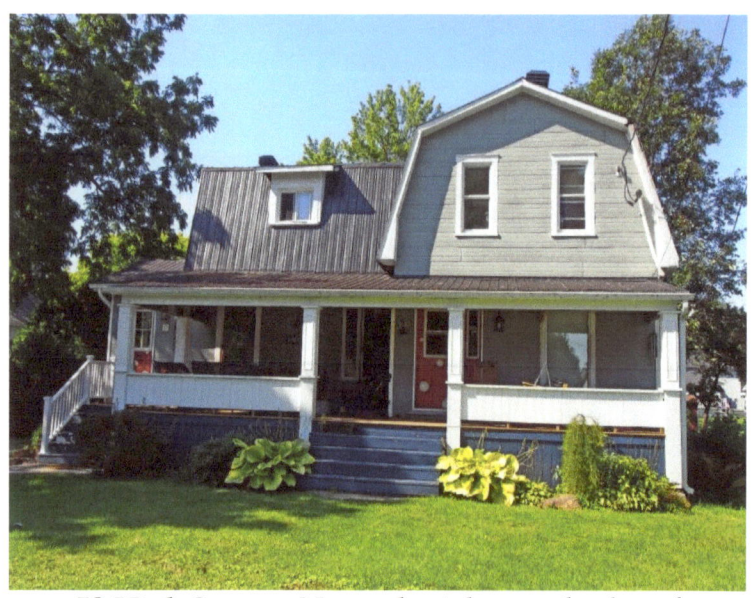

52 High Street – Neo-colonial – gambrel roof

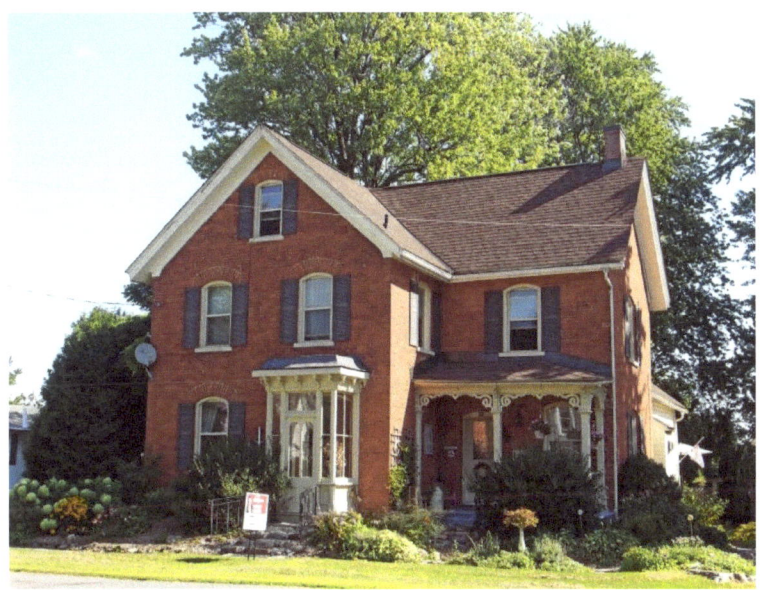

51 High Street – Victorian – voussoirs, ornate capital detailing on the veranda supports; enclosed front porch

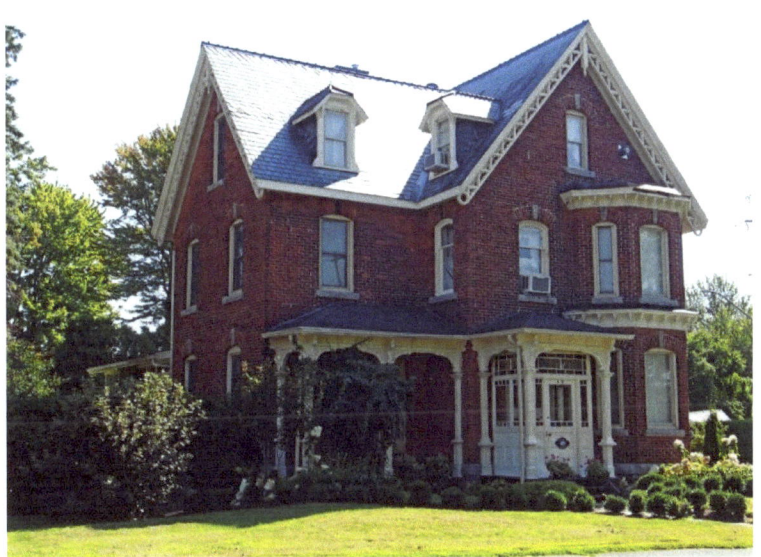

49 High Street – Gothic – steeply pitched gables with verge board and finials; dormers; two storey bay window with brackets; voussoirs and keystones; ornate pillars with decorative capitals; enclosed front entrance

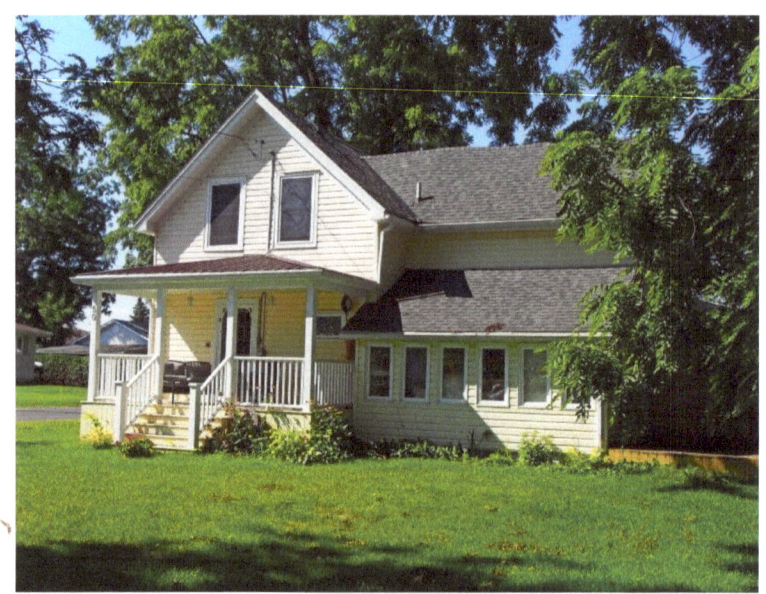

High Street

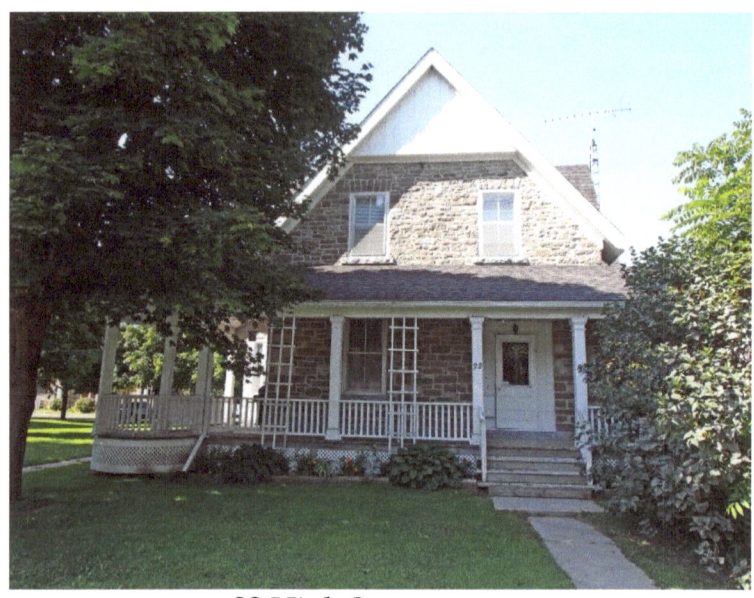

22 High Street - stone

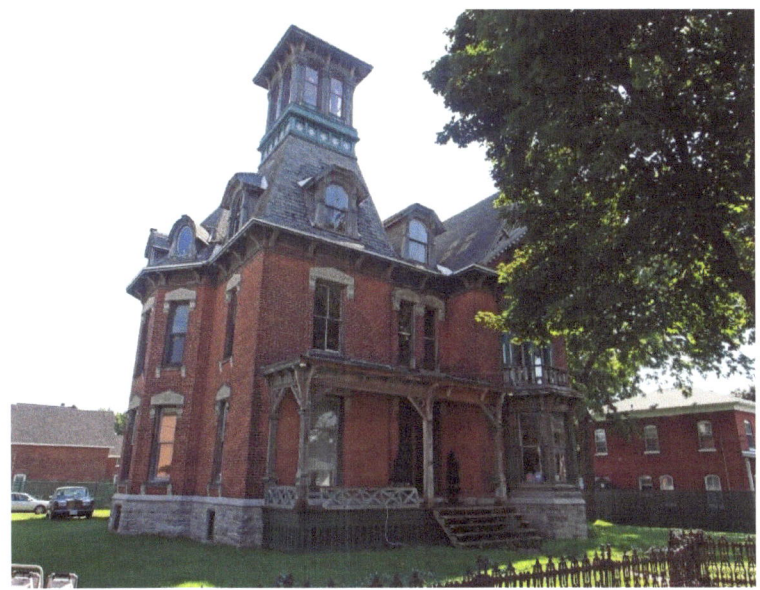

19 St. Lawrence Street – Italianate Villa – built 1876 – wrought iron fence; corner tower with its tall, four-sided lantern contains four pairs of Italianate round headed windows; classic Italianate porch and front door

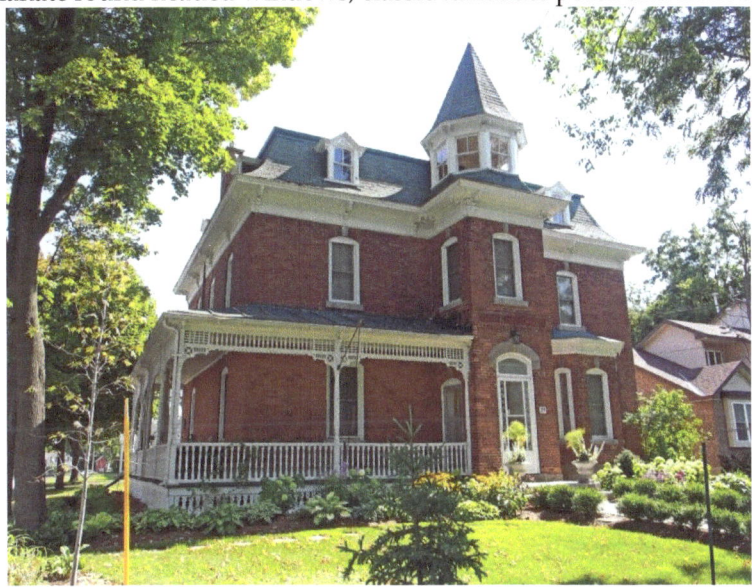

29 St. Lawrence Street – Second Empire – central tower directly above the front door topped with a belvedere; mansard roof with dormers

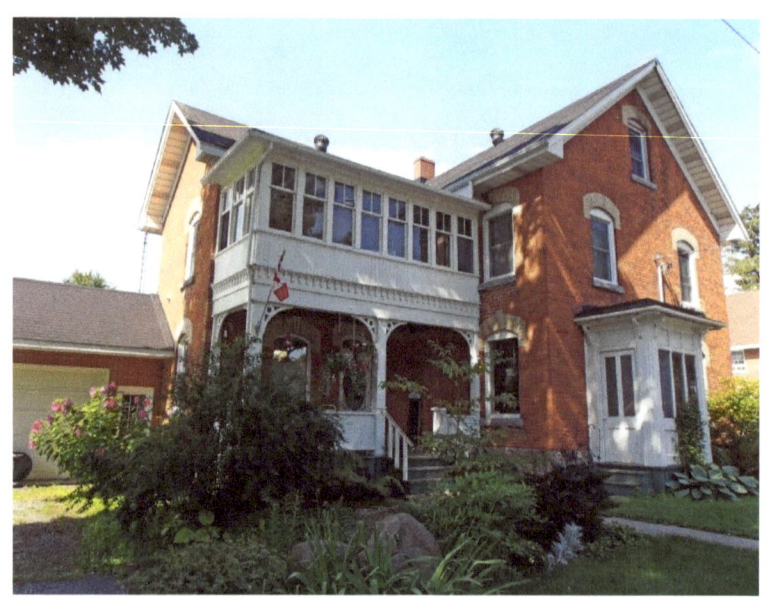

26 St. Lawrence Street

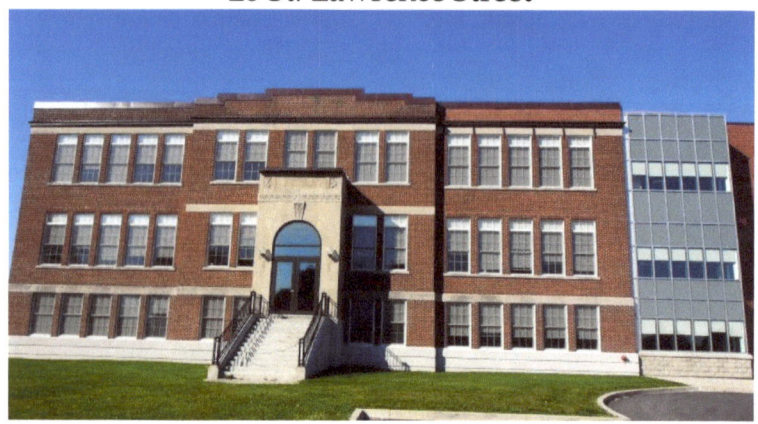

Ottawa Street – Morrisburg Collegiate Institute – first high school of Morrisburg started in 1864 – fire destroyed earlier building in 1925 – this building built in 1925 served the community for forty-one years, closing in 1967 when the Seaway was constructed – at that time it was amalgamated with the Iroquois Collegiate Institute and both student bodies were transferred to the new Seaway District High School in Iroquois

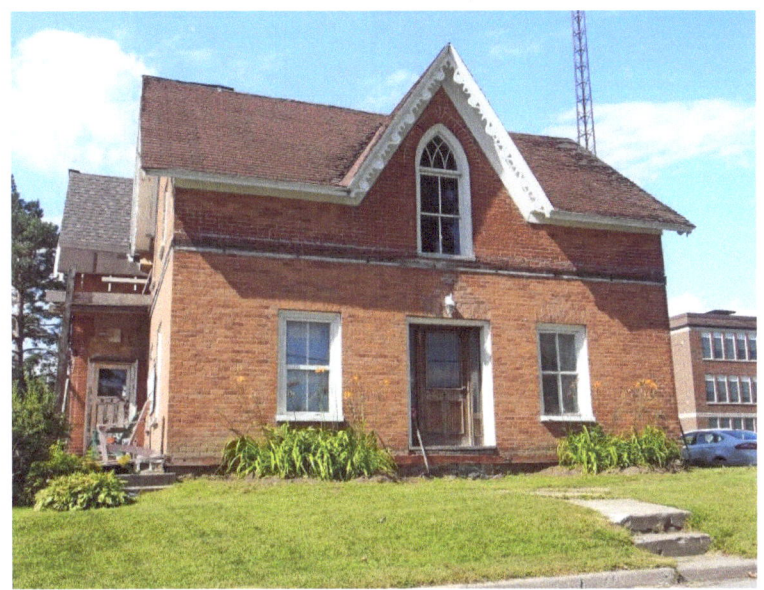

18 Ottawa Street – built 1881 – Gothic Revival style, verge board trim on gable

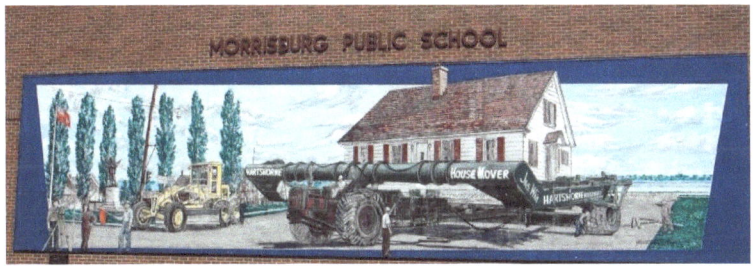

16 Second Street - Morrisburg Public School mural

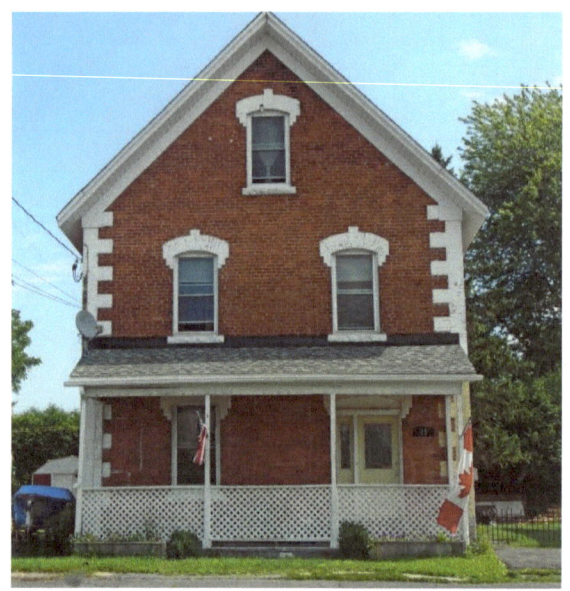

25 Ontario Street – Gothic, corner quoins

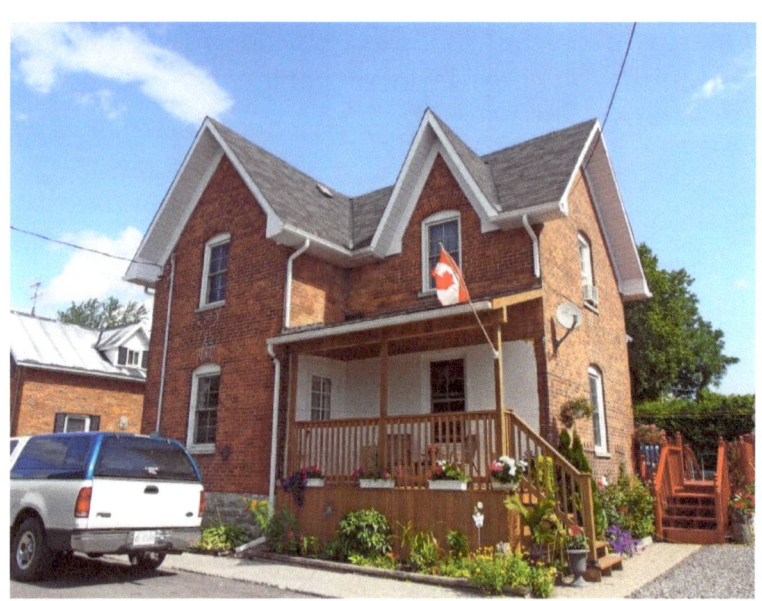

Ontario Street - Victorian

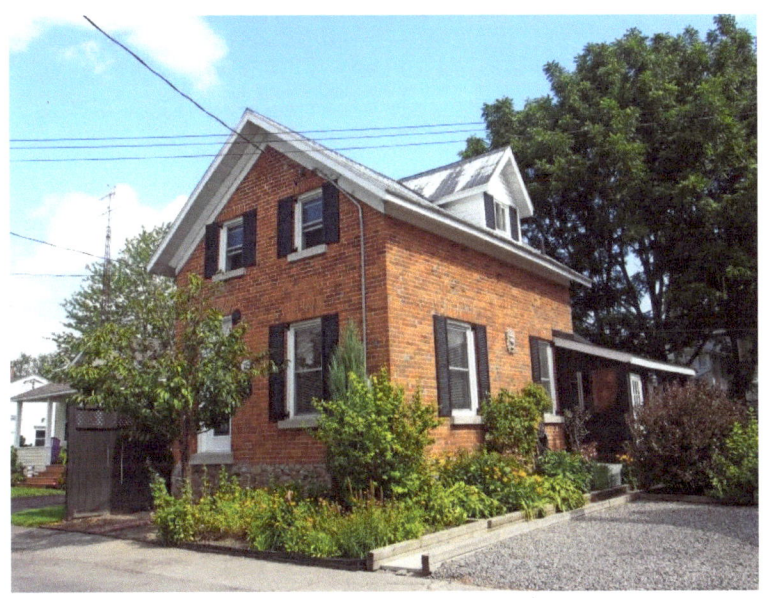

Ontario Street – Victorian, dormer

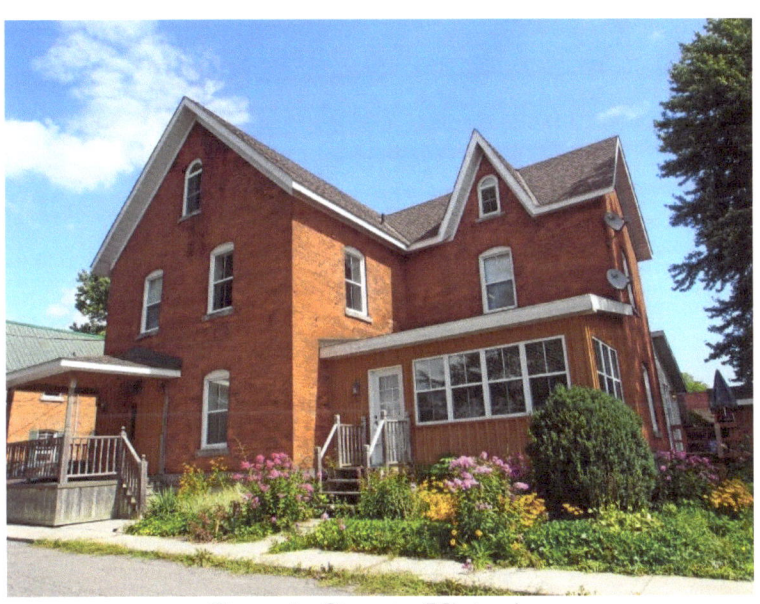

Ontario Street - Victorian

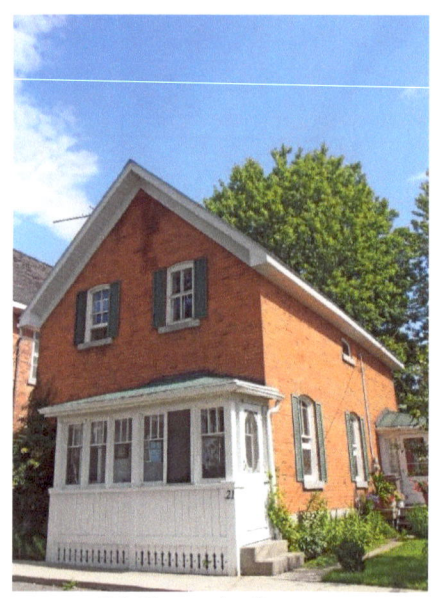

21 Ontario Street

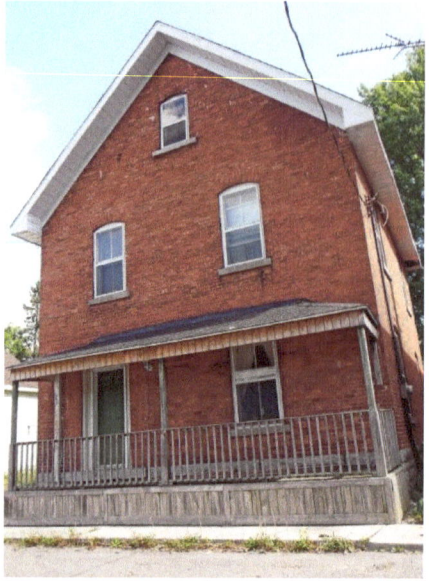

Ontario Street

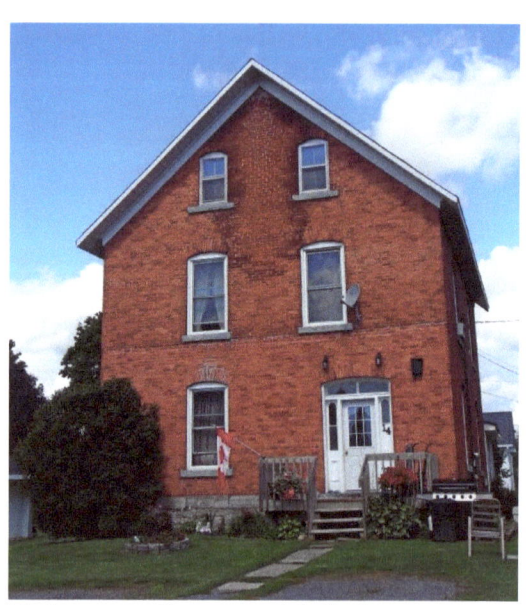

14 Annette Street – sidelights, transom

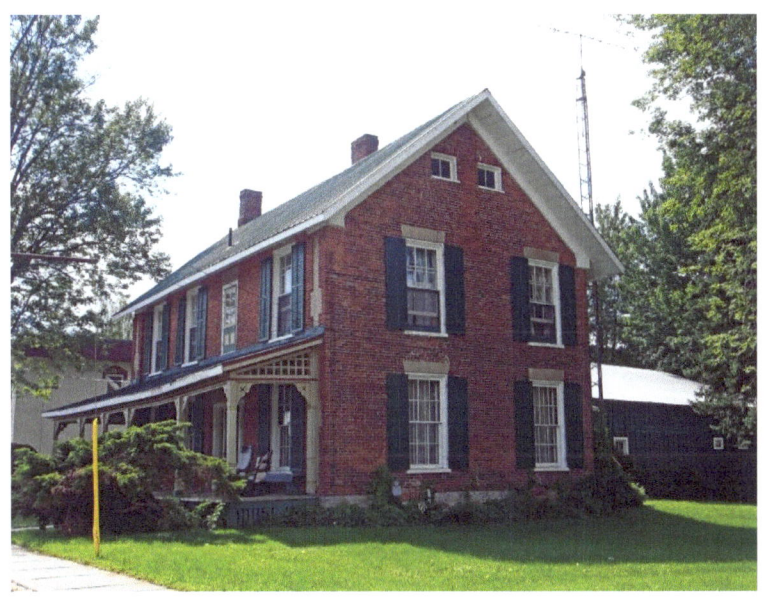

24 Sir James Morris Drive – Georgian – balanced façade,
decorative veranda support posts

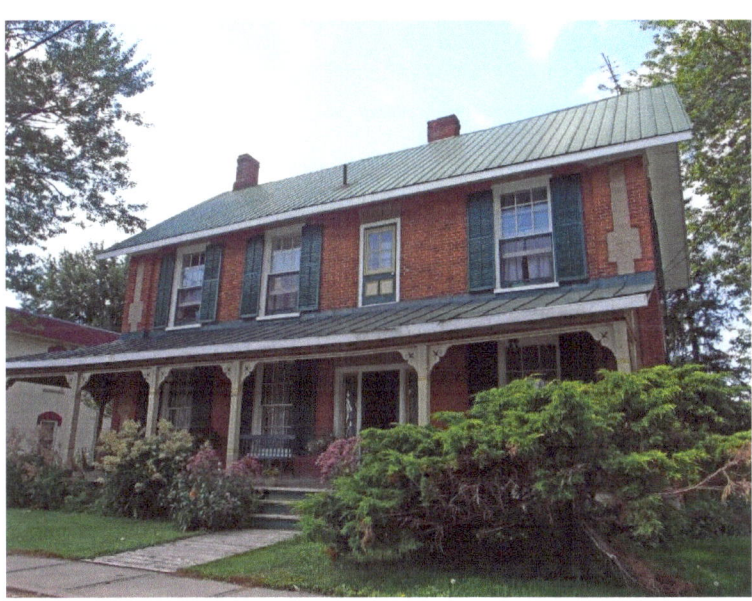

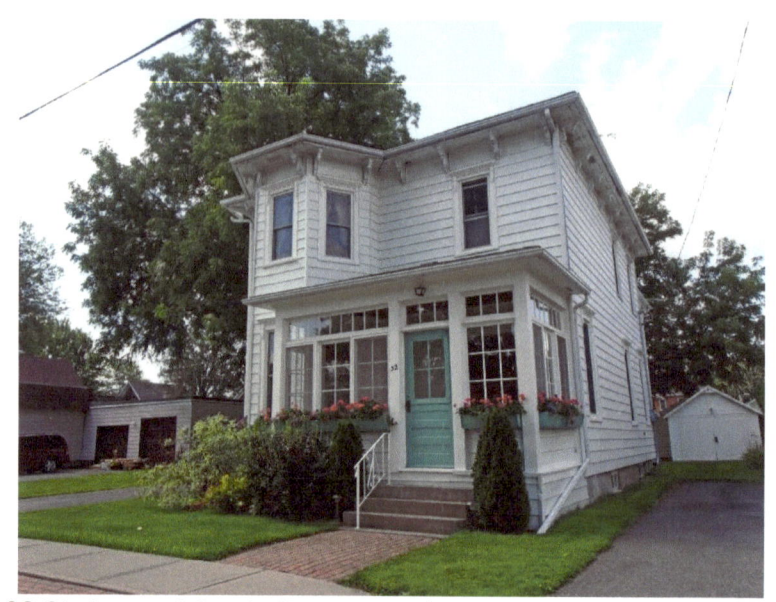

32 Sir James Morris Drive – Italianate – cornice brackets, enclosed front porch

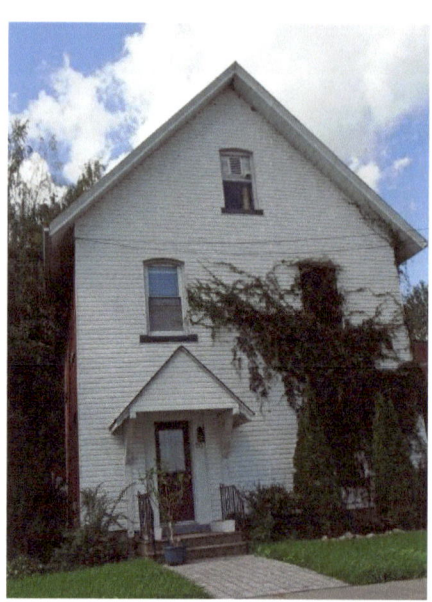

20 Sir James Morris Drive – Victorian, pediment

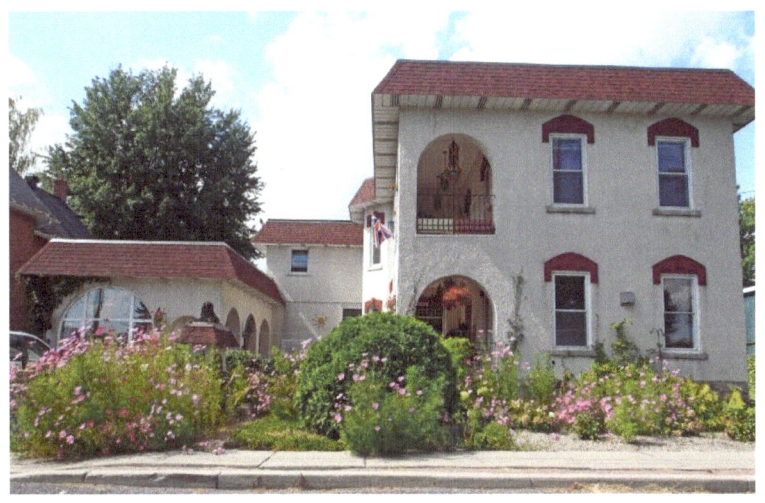

Sir James Morris Drive – stucco, wide cornice, decorative window lintels, Spanish style semi-circular openings

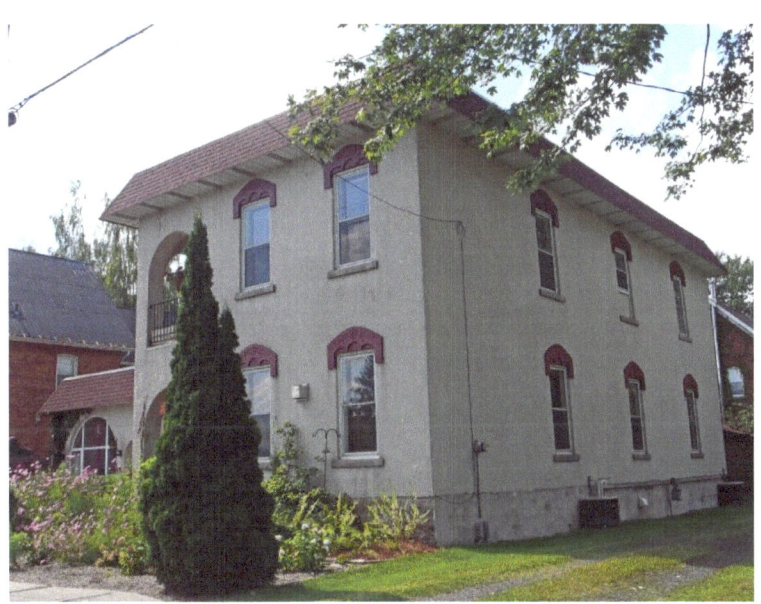

Architectural Terms

Bay Window: A window that projects out from a wall, in a semicircular, rectangular, or polygonal design. Used frequently in Gothic and Victorian designs. Example: 31 Lakeshore Drive, Page 10	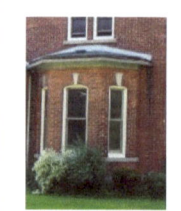
Belvedere: (from the Italian "beautiful view") an architectural feature on a roof, in a garden or on a terrace that gives a beautiful view. Example: 29 St. Lawrence Street, Page 37	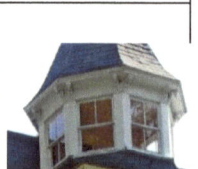
Brackets: a decorative or weight-bearing structural element which forms a right angle with one side against a wall and the other under a projecting surface such as an eave or roof. Example: 1 Augusta Street, Page 19	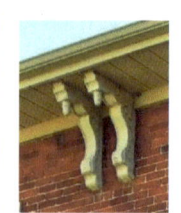
Buttress: a masonry structure built against or projecting from a wall which serves to support or reinforce the wall. In Canadian architecture, they are sometimes used for decoration. Example: Lakeshore Drive United Church, Page 8	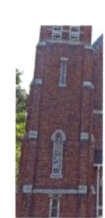

Columns were initially created to support a roof and porch structure. Originally they were free standing. Over time, builders began to build the walls between the columns so that the columns were part of the wall itself. These are called engaged columns. Engaged columns can be either structural or decorative. Example: 13 First Street, Page 24	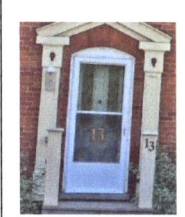
Dentil Moulding: an even series of rectangles used as ornamental decoration in cornices. Example: Knox Presbyterian Church, Page 25	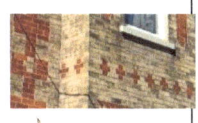
Dichromatic brickwork: the use of two colours of brick, tile or slate to decorate a façade. Example: 24 High Street, Page 29	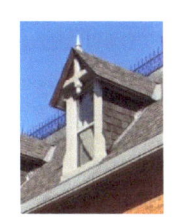
Dormer: (French for "sleep") a gable end window that pierces through the plane of a sloping roof surface to create usable space in the top floor or attic of a building by adding headroom. Example: 50 Lakeshore Drive, Page 15	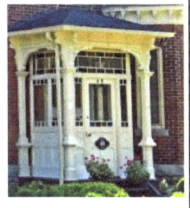
Entrance: The entrance encompasses the doorway and the inner vestibule or, in residential architecture, the covered porch. Example: 49 High Street, Page 35	

Gable: the triangular portion of a wall between the edges of a sloping roof. **Jacobean Gable:** the gable extends above the roofline. Example: 46 Lakeshore Drive, Page 14	
Gambrel Roof: a symmetrical two-sided roof with two slopes on each side; the upper slope is positioned at a shallow angle, while the lower slope is steep. It is similar to a mansard roof, but a gambrel has vertical gable ends instead of being hipped at the four corners of the building. Example: 52 High Street, Page 34	
Hipped Roof: a roof where all sides slope downwards to the walls with no gables. Example: Lakeshore Drive, Page 17	
Iron Cresting: A decorative ornament along the top of a roof. Iron cresting was popular in the Baroque era and also in Italianate, Victorian, Second Empire and Queen Anne styles of architecture. Example: 22 Lakeshore Drive, Page 9	
Keystones and Voussoirs: a voussoir is a wedge-shaped element used in building an arch. A keystone is the central stone that locks all the stones into position, allowing the arch to bear weight. A keystone is often enlarged and embellished. Example: 49 High Street, Page 35	

Lancet Window: a tall, narrow window with a pointed arch at its top. Example: Lakeshore Drive United, Page 8	
Lintel: horizontal part above a window or door that supports the structure above it. Example: Sir James Morris Drive, Page 45	
Mansard Roof: This style was popularized by Francois Mansart (1598-1666), an accomplished architect of the French Baroque period and especially fashionable during the Second French Empire (1852-1870). This roof is almost flat on the top section, with two slopes on each of its sides with the lower slope at a steeper angle than the upper and having dormer windows. Example: 22 Lakeshore Drive, Page 9	
Pediment: a triangular section above the door or portico, usually supported by columns. The inside of the triangle is called the tympanum. Example: 13 First Street, Page 24	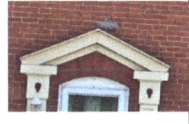

Pinnacle: is an architectural ornament originally forming the cap or crown of a buttress or small turret, but afterwards used on parapets at the corners of towers. The pinnacle looks like a small spire. It was mainly used in Gothic architecture. A pinnacle could be ornamental adding to its loftiness, or it could be structural as the pinnacles were very heavy with lead added to enable the flying buttresses to contain the stress of the structure vaults and roof. Example: 16 First Street, Page 22	
Quoin: masonry blocks at the corner of a wall, often a decorative feature, usually larger or of a different colour than the rest of the wall. Example: 25 Lakeshore Drive, Page 9	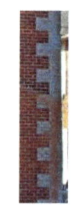
Rose Window: a circular window with ornamental tracery radiating from the centre. Example: St. James Anglican, Page 30	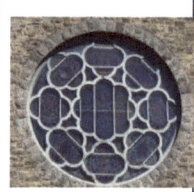

Sidelight: a vertical window that flanks a door, and is often used to emphasize the importance of a primary entrance. **Transom Window:** the light above the doorway, also called a fanlight. Example: First Street, Page 26	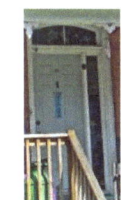
Tower: A circular, square, or octagonal vertical structure higher than the surrounding structure that is usually part of an existing building and is created either for extra defense or for a specific purpose such as a clock or a bell tower. Example: 19 St. Lawrence Street, Page 37	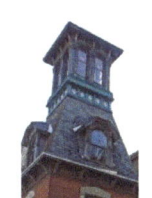
Verge board and Finial: also called bargeboards – hang from the projecting end of a roof and are often elaborately carved and ornamented. **Finial:** ornament added to the top of a gable, pinnacle, canopy or spire – a Gothic element. Example: 49 High Street, Page 35	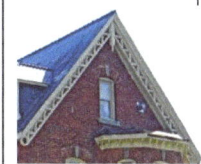
Window Hood: A **hood** is the piece found above window openings, usually of an ornate design, and covers the top third of the opening. Hoods are commonly placed above arched or curved openings on both windows and doors. Example: 22 Lakeshore Drive, Page 9	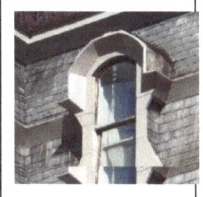

Building Styles

Georgian, before 1860 – This style began with the British King Georges in the 18th century. These buildings have balanced facades around a central door, medium-pitched gable roofs, and small paned windows. Example: 24 Sir James Morris Drive, Page 43	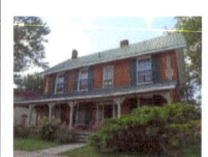
Gothic Revival, 1830-1890 – These decorative buildings have sharply-pitched gables with highly detailed verge boards, pointed-arch window openings, and dichromatic brickwork. It is a common style in Ontario. Example: 16 First Street, Page 22	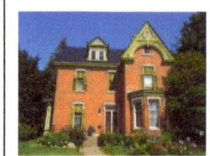
Italianate, 1850-1900 – A two story rectangular building with a mild hip roof, a projecting frontispiece, and generous eaves with ornate cornice brackets was the basis of the style; often there are large sash windows, quoins, ornate detailing on the windows, belvederes and wraparound verandahs. Italianate commercial buildings often have cast iron cresting and elegant window surrounds. Example: 48 Lakeshore Drive, Page 16	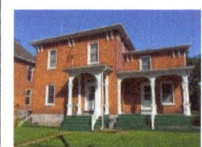

Italian Villa: This style was the first Ontario style that broke from the architectural traditions of the first settlers and imitated the harmony and balance of Classical architecture found in Northern Italian villas. The style is strictly residential and is characterized by an irregular roofline punctuated by a tall tower or campanile (bell tower). Small balconies, cantilevered eaves offering deep summer shade and arcaded porticos are standard features. Architects designing these houses were clearly after the picturesque. Example: 19 St. Lawrence Street, Page 37	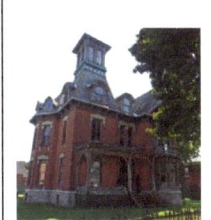
Neo-colonial (also Colonial Revival, Georgian Revival or Neo-Georgian) architecture seeks to revive elements of architectural style of American colonial architecture of the period around the Revolutionary War which drew strongly from Georgian architecture of Great Britain. Architecture from the 18th and early 19th centuries in Ontario includes a wide assortment of detailing and ornament applied to a design centered around the fireplace and the source of water. Structures are typically two stories, have a symmetrical front facade with elaborate front doorways, often with decorative crown pediments, fanlights, and sidelights, symmetrical windows flanking the front entrance, often in pairs or threes, and columned porches. Example: 52 High Street, Page 34	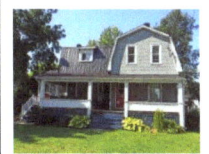

Queen Anne, 1885-1900 – This style is distinguished by an irregular outline featuring a combination of an offset tower, broad gables, projecting two-storey bays, verandahs, multi-sloped roofs, and tall, decorative chimneys. A mixture of brick and wood is common. Windows often have one large single-paned bottom sash and small panes in the upper sash. Example: 12 Lakeshore Drive, Page 6	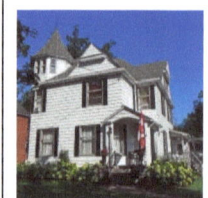
Second Empire, 1860-1880 – The mansard roof is the most noteworthy feature of this style and is evidence of the French origins. Projecting central towers and one or two-storey bays can also be present. Example: 31 Lakeshore Drive, Page 10	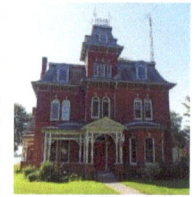
Vernacular/Traditional Mode 1638 - 1950 Influenced but not defined by a particular style, vernacular buildings are made from easily available materials and exhibit local design characteristics. Example: 17 Lakeshore Drive, Page 7	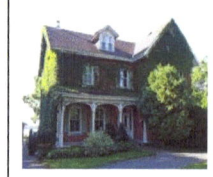
Victorian - In Ontario, a Victorian style building can be seen as any building built between 1840 and 1900 that doesn't fit into any of the other categories. It encompasses a large group of buildings constructed in brick, stone, and timber, using an eclectic mixture of Classical and Gothic motifs. Example: 34 Lakeshore Drive, Page 11	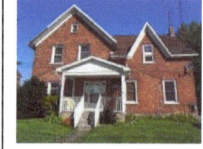

www.ingramcontent.com/pod-product-compliance
Lightning Source LLC
Chambersburg PA
CBHW040856180526
45159CB00001B/436